NAHUM ZEPHANIAH HABAKKUK

Minor Prophets of the Seventh Century B.C.

NAHUM
ZEPHANIAH
HABAKKUK

Minor Prophets
of the
Seventh Century B.C.

By

Hobart E. Freeman

MOODY PRESS
CHICAGO

Library of Congress Catalog Card Number: 72-95031
ISBN: 0-8024-2034-6

All scripture quotations in this book are from the American Standard Version. The term *Jehovah* is rendered "the Lord" throughout.

Printed in the United States of America

CONTENTS

INTRODUCTION TO THE SEVENTH CENTURY B.C. PROPHETS

THE SEVENTH CENTURY B.C. marks a critical period in the history of the Hebrew nation, as it is the prelude to the destruction of Jerusalem and the Babylonian captivity of the people of Judah. The prophet Daniel actually conducted his ministry while in captivity, having been carried to Babylon in the latter part of this century. The ministries of three of the minor prophets fall in this period: Nahum, Zephaniah, and Habakkuk.

The significance of the ministries of the three seventh century prophets under consideration lies in the nature of their message: their theme is *divine judgment*. Nahum is concerned with the approaching judgment of God upon Nineveh because of Assyria's destruction of the northern kingdom of Israel in 722 B.C., as well as for the city's wickedness and oppression. Zephaniah's message stresses the universal judgment of God in the day of the Lord, both upon Judah and the world in general. Habakkuk's prophecy is directed first against the kingdom of Judah because of her sin and apostasy, and then against the Chaldeans who destroyed Jerusalem and carried the inhabitants to Babylon.

Both Israel and Judah were strong and prosperous kingdoms during the early part of the previous century. But largely due to the introduction of idolatrous calf worship into Israel, the northern kingdom ignored the warnings of the prophets and embarked upon a road of apostasy which resulted in its destruction at the hands of the Assyrians in 722 B.C. (2 Ki 17). However, the lesson of Israel's judgment was lost upon Judah, who fell victim to the same sins that had overcome the northern kingdom.

It was in this context that the seventh century prophets were sent forth to proclaim their message of judgment against sin and the ultimate triumph of righteousness. Their message was one of judgment not only against Judah but also against the nations and would result in the purification of a remnant to carry out God's plan and purpose in history.

This enables us to understand the underlying significance of the use of prophecy concerning the heathen nations, such as Nahum's prophecy of judgment against Nineveh, and Habakkuk's prophecy against Babylon, as well as Zephaniah's message of universal or world judgment. Babylon, like Assyria who had earlier destroyed Israel, was temporarily to be God's instrument of chastisement upon Judah for her sins; nevertheless, both Assyria and Babylon would inevitably receive their punishment also. Thus, God's purpose in such prophecy was to demonstrate His universal sovereignty over all nations, which would at the same time give comfort and consolation to the faithful that wickedness and oppression would ultimately be overthrown and that righteousness would prevail throughout the earth.

PART ONE
NAHUM

1

INTRODUCTION TO NAHUM

The Prophet

The title, according to verse 1, designates Nahum, the Elkoshite, as the author of the prophecy. Nothing is known of the prophet Nahum outside the book itself. Traditions concerning his place of birth and ministry are, however, numerous. The prophet is called "the Elkoshite" (1:1), indicating that he was a native of Elkosh. Its location cannot be determined with certainty, although four sites have been proposed:

1. Elkosh is supposed by some to represent the modern village of Alkush on the Tigris River in Assyria (Iraq), where tradition locates the tomb of the prophet. Nahum's acquaintance with Nineveh (1:14; 2:5-6, 9), as well as his use of certain Assyrian words (2:7; 3:17), is said to lend support to the view that Nahum was a descendant of the inhabitants of the northern kingdom of Israel carried into exile by Sargon in 722 B.C. This tradition is quite late, however, arising long after the prophet's time. Moreover, the appearance of certain Assyrian terms and references in the prophecy are not unusual since Assyria was well known in the seventh century B.C. from her contacts with Palestine.
2. Some place Elkosh in Galilee, Jerome identifying it with

El Kauze. But the prophet's silence regarding the northern kingdom, and his mention of Judah, give little support to this theory.

3. Others identify it with Capernaum, which means city of Nahum. The original name according to this view was probably Elkosh, and was later changed to Capernaum in the prophet's honor.
4. Others suggest that Nahum was from the tribe of Simeon, and place Elkosh in the south of Judah (called either Elcesei or Bir el-kaus). The prophet's interest in the triumph of the southern kingdom (1:15) seems to favor this view, although the exact location of Elkosh is uncertain.

Nahum in Hebrew means comfort or consolation. His name may have symbolic reference to his message of comfort and consolation to Judah because of the Assyrian oppression, inasmuch as his theme in the approaching downfall of Nineveh. The Assyrians had not only destroyed the kingdom of Israel, but also presented a threat to Judah.

Among the minor prophets, Nahum is highly regarded by Old Testament expositors. His prophecy is an impressive poem comparable to Isaiah. The language is graphic and filled with colorful imagery. Nahum's subject is the downfall of Nineveh. The prophecy falls into three divisions: chapter 1 is an introductory psalm of triumph over the approaching fall of Nineveh; chapter 2 graphically describes the siege and destruction of the city itself; and chapter 3 gives the reasons for her downfall.

Period of Ministry

Assyria had been a terror in the Near Eastern world for

a considerable period. At the time of Nahum's prophecy the nation was at the height of its power. Nineveh's reputation for cruelty and ruthlessness was unsurpassed. The Assyrian empire, strong and formidable, had extended its control far and wide, subduing its enemies and humbling Judah who was compelled to pay annual tribute.

The date of Nahum's prophecy can be determined on the basis of the statement by the prophet in 3:8-10. Since Nahum refers to the fall of Thebes (No-amon), which occurred in 663 B.C., as a past event, the prophecy was subsequent to this time. Furthermore, the destruction of Nineveh which occurred in 612 B.C. is predicted as a future event; hence, the prophecy must have been delivered sometime between 663 and 612 B.C. Moreover, since no king is mentioned in the superscription, contrary to the usual practice in the prophetic books, it may point to the wicked reign of King Manasseh (686-642), whose name may have been purposely omitted, a thing unlikely if Josiah (640-609) had been occupying the throne of Judah. In view of all this, an approximate date of 650 B.C. is suggested for the prophecy of Nahum.[1]

Purpose of the Prophecy

The prophecy of Nahum as the superscription clearly asserts is concerned with one subject—the announcement of the imminent fall of Nineveh. In this regard the prophecy is like that of Jonah who also warned of Nineveh's overthrow. It is interesting that in the LXX (Septuagint) the book of Nahum immediately follows that of Jonah as being the complement of that book. In the previous century Jonah had preached a message of repentance, and the inhabitants of Nineveh had heeded his warning. Now, however, the nation has relapsed into its former wickedness and sin. As a consequence, Nahum announces the sentence of divine judgment upon the city, rebuking its arrogance, pride, oppression, and idolatry. As Keil notes, the prophecy exhibits such a close relationship to the kingdom of Judah that it may be looked upon as a prophecy of consolation and comfort to that kingdom.[2] However, the prophecy sets forth a timeless spiritual principle which is applicable to each succeeding generation from the time it was first delivered until the present. Nahum declares *the universal sovereignty of God,* and that *His administration extends over all the kingdoms of the earth.*

The righteous principles of His government embrace all nations. Nineveh is an object lesson to all rulers and kingdoms of the world. Assyria had more or less enjoyed the status of being the dominant empire of the Near East for centuries. Nineveh, the great city, was proud, idolatrous, and wicked. Moreover, she was seemingly invulnerable because of her power and fortifications. Her oppression and ruthlessness led her from one conquest to another, and in 722 B.C. she destroyed Israel and continued to oppress Judah. The message of Nahum reveals what God's uncompromising principles of righteousness will effect against a wicked and idolatrous nation. Its name will be cut off (1:4), and the nation destroyed (1:14). Kingdoms built on force and wickedness must eventually perish, whereas the sovereign kingdom of God will ultimately triumph in righteousness (1:2; 2:2).

The books of Jonah and Nahum comprise a single moral principle, revealing the two eternal aspects of divine righteousness: mercy and judgment God, in Jonah 3:10, is seen to be merciful and forgiving toward the penitent; but, as Nahum shows, He is unrelenting in His judicial wrath upon wickedness and oppression (3:1-8). This does not mean, however, that judgment is absent in Jonah's message, nor that mercy is not to be found in Nahum. On the contrary, toward those who trust in Him He is slow to anger (1:3) and a stronghold in the day of trouble (1:7), but against the sinful He is an avenger (1:2) full of wrath (1:2) and will not acquit the wicked (1:3).

Outline of Nahum

I. Nineveh's judgment announced, 1:1-15
  A. Divine wrath and mercy depicted, 1:1-7
    1. The avenging wrath of God upon the wicked, 1:2, 3b-6
    2. The mercy of the Lord toward the righteous, 1:3a, 7
  B. The overthrow of Nineveh predicted, 1:8-15
    1. Assyria to be destroyed, 1:8-12
    2. Judah to be delivered, 1:13
    3. Assyria's name to be blotted out, 1:14
    4. Jerusalem to rejoice, 1:15

II. Nineveh's destruction described, 2:1-13
  A. The siege of Nineveh, 2:1-10
    1. Attack preparation, 2:1
    2. His people restored, 2:2
    3. Nineveh assaulted, 2:3-10
  B. The devastated city, 2:11-12
    1. Nineveh to pass away, 2:11-12
    2. The certainty of Nineveh's overthrow, 2:13

III. Causes for Nineveh's destruction, 3:1-19
   A. God's indictment against Nineveh, 3:1-4
      1. Violence, deceit, and plunder, 3:1
      2. Ruthlessness and conquest, 3:2-3
      3. Idolatry, witchcraft, and slavery, 3:4
   B. Nineveh's downfall sealed, 3:5-19
      1. The humiliation of Nineveh, 3:5-6
      2. None lament for her, 3:7
      3. Her fate as certain as No-Amon's, 3:8-11
      4. Uselessness of Nineveh's defenses, 3:12-17
      5. Rejoicing over Nineveh's fall, 3:18-19

2

NINEVEH'S JUDGMENT ANNOUNCED
1:1-15

Divine Wrath and Mercy Depicted (1:1-7)

The theme of the prophecy of Nahum, like that of Jonah, is the fall of Nineveh. Chapter 1 is an introductory psalm of triumph over the impending destruction of that wicked city. Nahum depicts the Lord coming in judgment as a jealous God taking vengeance upon His enemies (1:1-6), but He will be "a stronghold in the day of trouble" to those who trust in Him (1:7).

VERSE 1

The prophecy has a twofold title. The first gives the *object* of the prophecy, "the burden of Nineveh," which would not otherwise be obvious merely from the book's contents; the second gives the *author* of the prophecy, "the book of the vision of Nahum."

"The burden of Nineveh": the term *burden* (the Hebrew word *massā'*, meaning load, burden, oracle) is generally used in the Old Testament of weighty, threatening prophecy (cf. Is 13:1; Hab 1:1). The term usually introduces a threat of judgment. The effect of Jonah's preaching had produced repentance temporarily over a century earlier. But now the Assyrians, as wicked and ruthless as ever, having destroyed the northern kingdom of Israel and threatening to do the same to Judah, fall under God's sentence of judgment.

VERSES 2-6

"The Lord is a jealous God and avengeth" (1:2): God had joined Israel to Himself as His wife in the exodus, and as her Husband He will bear no rival (Ex 20:5), nor permit His loved one to be oppressed. The threefold repetition of the term *avenge* in this verse is intended to emphasize this fact. "He reserveth wrath for his enemies": although God may withhold His judgment against sin for a time, this does not imply that He has forgotten, but only that He is slow to anger (v.3). The Scriptures depict God as long-suffering and merciful, as He proved Himself upon Nineveh's repentance over a century earlier; but they also reveal that He is inflexible in justice, and has a set time for dealing with the sins of the wicked and unrepentant (2 Pe 2:9; 3:8-10), for He "will by no means clear the guilty" (1:3b; cf. Ex 34:7).

There follows in verses 3b-6 a description of God's power and wrath in judgment as exhibited in His control over the forces of nature. This description of God's majesty and power is drawn from the revelation of Himself during the Exodus and runs throughout the Psalms (Ex 19:16-18; Judg 5:1-5; Ps 18; 97; Mic 1:2-7).

His vengeance shall sweep away the Assyrians like a "whirlwind" or a "storm" (v.3b), two of the most awesome and fearful of nature's destructive forces. The wrath of the Lord is depicted by the prophet as a tempestuous storm sweeping over the earth, the angry "clouds" swirling as dust under His feet as He descends from the heavens in judgment (v.3b). As evidence of His omnipotence (v.4), the

Lord "rebuketh the sea," as in Israel's passage through the Red Sea (Ex 14:21), and "drieth up all the rivers," as seen in the miracle at the Jordan (Jos 3). "Bashan . . . Carmel . . . and the flower of Lebanon languisheth (v.4): these regions noted for their fertility, trees, or vineyards will wither at the word of the Lord. "The mountains quake at him" (v.5): even the emblems of stability and permanence tremble before Him. Therefore, "Who can stand before his indignation?" asks the prophet (v.6): the question has already been answered in the foregoing description of God's judicial wrath, as expressed in the convulsions and upheavals in nature.

VERSE 7

"A stronghold in the day of trouble": the prophet assures the people of Judah of their deliverance from the Assyrian threat, announcing Nineveh's imminent destruction in verse 8. The overthrow of Nineveh at the hands of the Medes, Babylonians and Scythians occurred in 612 B.C., just a few years after Nahum's prophetic announcement. "He knoweth them that take refuge in him": as in Psalm 1:6, where we are informed that "the Lord knoweth the way of the righteous; but the way of the wicked shall perish," the meaning in Nahum 1:7 is not that God does not have any knowlege of the wicked, but that He does not know them redemptively as His children. This divine knowledge which God has concerning those whom He loves is an intimate, personal knowledge, such as exists, for instance, between a husband and wife or parent and child. It is knowledge resulting from the inseparable bond and attachment which exists between the heavenly Father and His children, expressing itself in loving care and protection (cf. 2 Ti 2:15-19; Ho 13:5; Amos 3:2).

The Overthrow of Nineveh Predicted (1:8-15)

God, declares Nahum, will make a full end of Nineveh, utterly consuming her as dry stubble. In days past there went out of Nineveh one who planned evil against the Lord and His people (King Sennacherib). Although the enemy came in full strength, the Lord cut them down, destroying the Assyrian host (2 Ki 19:35-37). Now the Lord intends to break the yoke of Assyria from off Judah. Nineveh's name will be blotted out, and God will dig her grave, at which time Judah will rejoice in the good tidings. In this passage we have a remarkably accurate prediction concerning Nineveh's downfall, as subsequent history confirms.

VERSE 8
"With an over-running flood he will make a full end of her place": Archaeological records seem to indicate that a vital part of the walls of Nineveh was destroyed by an unusually heavy flood of the Tigris River, thus permitting the enemy to force its way through this breach and storm the city (see 2:6 for further comments).

VERSE 9
"What do ye devise against the Lord? he will make a full end": this prediction which was certainly fulfilled in Assyria's complete destruction. "Affliction shall not rise up the second time": the Assyrians were never permitted a "second" victory over the Jews, and thus, by divine intervention, were never allowed to overthrow Judah as they had the northern kingdom of Israel.

VERSE 10
"For entangled like thorns, and drunken as with their drink, they are consumed utterly as dry stubble": the accounts from secular history concerning the downfall of Nineveh

relate how the Assyrians, whose army was attacked outside the walls of the city, regarded themselves as invincible after repeatedly repulsing the enemy, and gave themselves to excessive drinking and revelry. While so occupied they were surprised by the forces of the enemy and were overcome, the heavy flood later giving the besiegers access to the city itself after destroying a portion of the walls.

VERSE 11

"There is one gone forth out of thee, that deviseth evil against the Lord, that counselleth wickedness": God addresses Nineveh here. The reference is doubtless to the Assyrian King Sennacherib, who, several years previously, had come against the kingdom of Judah during the reign of Hezekiah. The historical account of this impious threat and wicked counsel of Sennacherib is recorded in 2 Kings 18-19.

VERSE 12

"Thus saith the Lord: Though [they were in] full strength, and likewise many, even so they have been cut down, and he has passed [away]": this is a literal translation of the Hebrew. The verbs in verses 11 and 12 in the Hebrew indicate the action is past or completed (the state of perfected action), whereas the versions erroneously suggest the future tense. The reference in these two verses is to an event already past at the time of Nahum's prophecy. In verse 12 we seem to have a clear reference to the supernatural annihilation of Sennacherib's army by the angel of the Lord when the Assyrian king came against Jerusalem:

> And it came to pass that night, that the angel of the Lord went forth, and smote in the camp of the Assyrians a hundred fourscore and five thousand: and when men arose early in the morning, behold, these were all dead

> bodies. So Sennacherib king of Assyria departed, and went and returned, and dwelt at Nineveh. And it came to pass as he was worshipping in the house of Nisroch his god, that Adrammelech and Sharezer smote him with the sword: and they escaped into the land of Ararat. And Esarhaddon his son reigned in his stead. (2 Ki 19:35-37)

VERSE 13
"And now will I break his yoke from off thee, and will burst thy bonds in sunder": this is doubtless a reference to the vassalage of Judah to Assyria; the Lord later broke this yoke in His overthrow of the Assyrian nation. King Hezekiah had paid tribute to Sennacherib when the Assyrian king had conquered Judah's fortified cities (2 Ki 18:14). Furthermore Manasseh, who reigned after him, had been overcome by the Assyrians and carried captive to Babylon (2 Ch 33:11).

VERSE 14
"No more of thy name be sown . . . I will make thy grave": it is predicted here that Nineveh's name would be blotted out and become extinct, and that the Lord would dig her grave, thus consigning this powerful nation to oblivion. This is confirmed in Ezekiel 32:22-23, where the prophet states that Assyria has been cast down into Sheol (place of departed spirits). He writes:

> Asshur [Assyria] is there [in Sheol] and all her company; her graves are round about her; all of them slain, fallen by the sword; whose graves are set in the uttermost parts of the pit, and her company is round about her grave; all of them slain, fallen by the sword, who caused terror in the land of the living.

This prophecy was literally fulfilled. So completely did

God bury Nineveh that every trace of the wicked city's existence disappeared for centuries, and even its site was lost to memory, causing some critics of the Bible to view the biblical references to Nineveh with skepticism. It was not until 1845, when Layard identified the site known as Kuyunjik as the ancient city of Nineveh, that the grave of this once powerful city came to light.

VERSE 15

"Behold, upon the mountains the feet of him that bringeth good tidings, that publisheth peace": the good tidings of peace over which Judah is encouraged to rejoice follow in the last half of this verse; it is the prophet's announcement of the imminent overthrow of their cruel oppressor Nineveh. The "mountains" are those about Jerusalem upon which the Assyrian host under Sennacherib had encamped not too many years previously, preventing Judah from keeping her feasts and conducting her worship freely. But when the messengers soon come announcing the destruction of Nineveh, then Judah will rejoice over the "good tidings."

This verse is almost identical with a prophecy in Isaiah 52:7 referring to a similar deliverance to come about a century later, when the Israelites would return from their captivity in Babylon in 536 B.C. (cf. Is 40:9). Nahum's prophecy (1:15), according to the apostle Paul in Romans 10:15, is also typical of our *spiritual deliverance* from bondage to Satan, when we believe the "good tidings" heralded by the ministers of the gospel that the kingdom of our oppressor (Satan) has been overthrown.[1]

3

NINEVEH'S DESTRUCTION DESCRIBED
2:1-13

The Siege of Nineveh (2:1-10)

THE ASSAULT against the city of Nineveh resulting in its downfall is graphically portrayed in chapter 2. Nineveh is depicted as anxiously making preparations for the attack because "he that dasheth in pieces is come" (2:1). The furious onslaught of the destroying army is vividly described: bloody shields, flashing swords and spears, and racing chariots in the streets. The enemy leaps up the wall and throws open the river gates; the palace is dissolved (2:2-6). The defenders of the city flee in panic, its inhabitants are carried into captivity, and the proud city is plundered and destroyed (2:7-10).

VERSE 1

The prophet addresses Nineveh, forewarning her of the siege she is about to undergo. "He that dasheth in pieces is come up against thee": here is meant the alliance of the Medes, Babylonians, and Scythians, who will act as God's "battle-axe" against Nineveh and "break in pieces" His enemies. Jeremiah 51:20 applies the same term to Nebuchadnezzar, God's instrument of judgment against the nations, including Judah (cf. also Jer 50:23, "the hammer of the whole earth"). Ironical advice by the prophet follows:

"Watch the way"—by which the enemy will come; "make thy loins strong"—the loins are regarded as the seat of strength. To "gird up thy loins," a relatively common phrase in Scripture, is to prepare or strengthen oneself for some task or conflict (cf. Job 38:3; 1 Pe 1:13).

VERSE 2

"For the Lord restoreth the excellency of Jacob, as the excellency of Israel": the KJV incorrectly renders this verse, "hath turned away the excellency of Jacob." The ASV corrects this, however, translating the Hebrew *shûv* as "restore." The prophet does not intend a distinction between the southern and northern kingdoms by use of these two names, Jacob and Israel, but both names stand here for the whole of Israel, as in Romans 11:26 where the apostle uses both terms to signify the one nation and its restoration.

God foretold through the prophet Isaiah also how He would use Assyria to chasten Israel for her sins (Is 10:5-11), and how that when He had accomplished this He would then in turn punish Assyria for her oppression of His people (Is 10:12-14), after which Israel would be restored (Is 10:20-27).

VERSES 3-10

In this section appears a description of the fearsome assault against Nineveh. The first furious onslaught of the enemy (2:3-6) is followed by the captivity of the people (2:7), the flight of Nineveh's defenders (2:8), and finally the plunder of the city itself (2:9-10).

"The shield of his mighty men is made red" (v.3): the shields of the ancient soldiers were of various shapes and materials, at times consisting of a wooden frame covered with leather, which some suggest were dyed red to strike terror in their enemies; others were covered with brass or copper, which when shone upon by the sun may have caused the redness spoken of by the prophet. On the other hand, it may refer to blood from their enemies upon their shields, denoting the fierceness of the slaughter. Red in Scripture often signifies judgment (cf. Is 63:1-6; Zec 1:8; Rev 6:4). Scarlet was a favorite color of military and battle dress (cf. Mt 27:28). "The chariots flash with steel:" literally, the Hebrew reads, "the chariots are with the fire of steel," signifying the glittering and flashing of their steel ornaments and fittings, as well as the metal rims of the wheels striking sparks from the stones over which they pass. The simile is continued in the next verse where we are told that "the appearance of them is like torches" (2:4), speaking of the gleaming flashes reflected from the chariots darting to and fro in the streets, as well as from the shields and armor of their occupants. Writings from the second century B.C. make an interesting reference to this effect: "Now when the sun shone upon the shields of gold and brass, the mountains glittered therewith, and shined like lamps of fire" (1 Mac 6:39).

Verse 5 describes the preparation for attack upon the city. "He remembereth his nobles": some expositors believe this to be a reference to the king of Assyria who turns his attention to his leaders, sending them forth to defend the walls of Nineveh and repel the attack. In their haste and fear, the hard-pressed leaders stumble about confused and bewildered as they make their way through the city.[1] However, it is more consistent with the context in chapter 2, which depicts the enemies' assault upon Nineveh, to apply this verse to the besiegers who stumble in their haste to assault the walls of the city. The phrase "he remembers his nobles," as the next clause indicates, idiomatically expresses the command for the assaulting military leaders to prepare the siege weapons for an attack upon the walls of the city.

"The mantelet is prepared": the Hebrew term means literally a "covering" or "protection," erected to protect the besiegers of the city's walls from the stones, spears, and arrows of the defenders of Nineveh. Ancient weapons, contrary to popular opinion, were not always mere primitive devices such as the bow and spear, but many weapons and instruments of warfare had been devised, some of which were quite effective in overcoming defenses and gaining access to a city or fortress. In 2 Chronicles 26:11-15, for example, we are told of great "engines" of war invented by skillful men for King Uzziah which were designed "to shoot arrows and great stones." The engines could throw stones weighing from fifty to three hundred pounds. Arrows of varying sizes could be launched from these devices, their range exceeding one-fourth mile. Huge battering rams, suspended in portable towers, often on wheels, were used to make a breach in the wall of a city.[2]

According to Layard the battering rams were of several kinds. Some were attached to movable towers which held warriors and armed men. These towers were then placed before the walls of the besieged city, and constituted a fort. We are informed in Jeremiah 52:4 that "Nebuchadnezzar king of Babylon came, he and all his army, against Jerusalem, and encamped against it; and they built forts against it round about." Ezekiel also alludes to this military practice. To portray symbolically the coming assault upon Jerusalem, God commanded the prophet to "lay siege against it, and build forts against it, and cast up a mound against it; set camps also against it, and plant battering rams against it round about" (Eze 4:2). Archers on the walls shot arrows against the towers, while others hurled stones or sought to destroy the battering rams with fire by hurling lighted torches against them. The besiegers also employed the use of long staffs with an iron head, which were used to force stones from the walls, while catapults hurled stones and darts over the walls. Efforts were made to set fire to the gates of the city, and troops attempted to scale the walls with assault ladders, while archers below kept the enemy upon the walls from overturning them. The warriors were protected by large shields of wickerwork, sometimes covered with hides, which concealed the entire person (a form of mantelet, 2:5).[3]

"The gates of the rivers are opened, and the palace is dissolved" (v.6): this is a reference (as in 1:8) to the fact that the capture of Nineveh was due to divine intervention in the form of an unprecedented flood, which destroyed a large part of the wall, thus giving the enemy access to the city. This was no doubt accomplished by direct action of the Tigris River against the wall of the city, since Nineveh was built on its eastern bank. Some suggest, however, that the "gates of the rivers" were the gates of the city which were situated down by the river which the enemy broke open; others believe this is a reference to the gates which controlled the Khoser River which flowed directly through the city of Nineveh. However, the reference is probably figurative, "the gates of the rivers" signifying the overwhelming flood which inundated Nineveh (similar to the metaphorical expression, "the windows of heaven," Gen 7:11).

The phrase "the palace is dissolved" may also denote the destruction of the royal palace by the action of water, or may have reference to its devastation by fire. Ancient historians record the tradition concerning the death of the king of Assyria. It is said that in his despondency because of the breach made in the walls by the flood and despairing of any means of escape he constructed in his palace an immense funeral pyre from its furnishings. He then placed upon it his gold and silver and burned himself to death in order to avoid falling alive into the enemy's hands. The city of Nineveh itself was then pillaged and burned by the besiegers who completely destroyed the walls of the city.[4]

"And it is decreed: she is uncovered, she is carried away" (v.7): the KJV and ASV margin translate "it is decreed" as a proper noun, "Huzzab," meaning "fixed" or "established," thus taking the Hebrew word as an epithet for the name of the queen of Nineveh, or (more likely) as a symbolical name for Nineveh itself, who is to be carried away captive to Babylon. The term in its verbal form means "to stand" or "be established," from which the ASV derives "it is decreed." However, it seems best to follow the marginal reading here (as the Hebrew authorities suggest), taking Huzzab as an appellative and render the verse: "And Huzzab (i.e., Nineveh, the securely established city) is uncovered (conquered), she is carried away." Symbolical names for cities or nations are not infrequent in Scripture (e.g., *Zion,* meaning "citadel," or *Ariel,* meaning "lion of God," both signifying Jerusalem; *Dumah,* meaning "silence," for Edom, perhaps referring to its coming destruction in Is 21:11-12; cf. Ob 15-16).

"But Nineveh hath been from of old like a pool of water: yet they flee away" (v.8): this is an allusion to her invulnerable position, situated beside the Tigris River, and encompassed as an island surrounded by a pool of water; nevertheless, her inhabitants will be forced to flee before the enemy. "Stand, stand," the leaders will cry to her defenders; but Nahum declares that "none looketh back!" The cause for such terror and panic upon the city's inhabitants is graphically portrayed in the opening verses of this chapter (vv.1-6).

"Take ye the spoil. . . . She is empty, and void, and waste" (vv.9-10): upon the flight of the city's defenders, Nineveh is pillaged. The prophet calls for the invaders to come and gather the rich spoil, which was immense. Sinsharishkun, King of Nineveh at the time of its fall, is reputed to have placed 150 golden beds and over 100 tables of gold, as well as gold and silver vases and ornaments in great quantities, together with rich rainment upon his funeral pyre, before consigning himself to the flames. Countless millions of dollars in gold, silver, ivory, as well as other treasures were taken from the city by its spoilers in almost unlimited quantities just as the prophet foretold: "Take ye the spoil of silver, take the spoil of gold; for there is no end of the store, the glory [wealth] of all goodly furniture" (v.9): Nineveh's wealth arose from its own plunder and the annual tribute exacted from subject nations, as well as its vast trade (Eze 27:23-24). Now nothing would remain, for "she is empty, and void, and waste" (v.10).

On the Babylonian Chronicle, an ancient clay tablet now in the British Museum, there is an actual record of the fall of Nineveh, which confirms Nahum's prophecy. Showing remarkable similarity to the statements in chapter 2, the account states:

> "A mighty assault was made upon the city. In the month of Abu, the city was taken. A great slaughter was made of the people and nobles. . . . Great quantities of spoil from the city, beyond counting, they carried off. The city they turned into a mound and ruin heap. The army of Assyria deserted."[5]

The Devastated City (2:11-13)

Nahum in these verses ironically contrasts the devastated city with its former glory and power.

VERSE 11

"Where is the den of the lions?" he asks. In 1:8 the prophet had declared that God would make "a full end of her place," and, furthermore, that He would dig her grave (1:14), a prophecy so literally fulfilled that even the site of the city disappeared from history. The image of the lion which the prophet uses to depict Assyria is appropriate, because sculptured lions were frequently stationed at the gates of temples and palaces to act as guardians, and because of the lion's cruel, ravenous nature. Nineveh, moreover, was filled with the spoil of many nations, as a lion's den is of its prey.

At the time of Nahum's prophecy, Assyria was at the height of its power and glory. Nineveh, its capital, is first mentioned in Genesis 10:11 as founded by Nimrod; and by the time of Jonah (782 B.C.) who prophesied there, it was designated as "that great city" (Jon 1:2; 3:2). Nineveh became one of the royal residences of Assyria after the twelfth century B.C. and later, under Sennacherib, was made the capital of Assyria. In the time of Nahum, Assyria had extended its conquests westward to the Mediterranean Sea and into Palestine and Egypt. The nation of Israel was well acquainted with the oppression of the Assyrians from past experience. In the battle of Karkar, Shalmaneser III had defeated a coalition of twelve kings, among whom was Ahab, King of Israel. This Assyrian monarch, on a later campaign, exacted heavy tribute from Jehu of Israel (841-814 B.C.); and Tiglath-Pileser III (744-727 B.C.) overran the kingdom of Israel and deported many of its inhabitants to Assyria (2 Ki 15:29). Later the Assyrian ruler, Shalmaneser V, laid siege to Samaria which fell in 722 B.C. to his successor, Sargon II. The northern kingdom of Israel ceased to exist upon the downfall of Samaria, its inhabitants being carried captive to Assyria (2 Ki 17). After the death of Sargon II, his son Sennacherib invaded Palestine and conquered several fortified cities of Judah, exacting a heavy tribute from King Hezekiah of Judah (2 Ki 18:13f.).

Sennacherib had done much to increase the strength and magnificence of Nineveh, building great temples, palaces, and fortifications. Nineveh was confident in her apparent invulnerablity; but Nahum, rebuking her pride, cruelty, and wickedness, proclaimed her imminent and permanent destruction. In a few short years after his prophecy (c.650 B.C.) her final end came. A coalition of Medes, Babylonians, and Scythians besieged the city. The siege continued for some time, as the fortifications of Nineveh were too formidable for the battering machines of the enemy. The Assyrian king, having repulsed several attacks by the enemy, was under no apprehension concerning his attackers, confiding, it is said, in an ancient oracle which predicted that Nineveh would never fall until the "river" became its enemy.

Later, however, when the rains fell in such abundance that the waters of the Tigris River overflowed and inundated the city, destroying one of its walls for a great distance and giving the enemy access to the city itself, the king became convinced that the oracle was fulfilled. Despairing of any means of escape he destroyed himself on a great funeral pyre in his palace. In 612 B.C. Nineveh fell to the besiegers who pillaged the city of its vast treasures (2:9-10), and then burned it to the ground. The attackers did not leave anything standing in the city that had been dominant over the Near East for so long. They razed its houses, temples, palaces, and its fortifications to the ground. So effectively did God dig her grave and bury her (1:14) that every trace of Nineveh's existence disappeared for over 2000 years and even its site was unknown. History has no other example of so complete a destruction of so great a city. When Alexandar the Great fought nearby, he was not aware that the once magnificent city of Nineveh lay buried at his feet. All traces of the great Assyrian empire had disappeared.

VERSE 12

"The lion did tear in pieces enough for his whelps, and strangled for his lionesses": the figure of the ravenging lion is continued in this verse. The Assyrian nation provided for its people by plundering other nations. The phrase "his lionesses" doubtless refers to the king's wives and concubines. It was an ancient custom for ruling monarchs to assign certain cities or provinces to their favorite wives, which, together with plundered riches, became their prey (cf. 2 Mac 4:30).

VERSE 13

"Behold, I am against thee, saith the Lord": with this, Nineveh's downfall is pronounced. The cruel oppressor of the nations is soon to be overthrown. For Nahum, Nineveh is the representative of all worldly dominion in antagonism against God. He enunciates the immutable spiritual principle that kingdoms built upon tyranny and wickedness will ultimately be overthrown as a consequence of God's judicial righteousness. The prophet seeks to show, therefore, that the overthrow of Nineveh is not man's work (even though by his instrumentality), but that it is to occur by supernatural intervention, for it will be destroyed at the very height of its power and prosperity. Nineveh was a city of blood, a dwelling place of ravenous beasts which had preyed upon other nations with unparalleled cruelty and violence. Now, declares the prophet, this violence is to be brought to bear upon her, for "he that dasheth in pieces is come up against thee" (2:1; cf. Mt 7:2).

"The voice of thy messengers shall no more be heard": the messengers of Nineveh stand in contrast with the messengers of Zion described in 1:15. Whereas the messengers of Nineveh carried news of that wicked city's conquests and oppression of the other nations, those of Zion brought "good tidings," and published news of "peace." For an example of the wicked counsel of one of Assyria's messengers, note Rabshekeh's defiant address against God and King Hezekiah in 2 Kings 18:19-37. The Assyrian messenger spoke of strife and contention, whereas Isaiah prophesied assurance to King Hezekiah, promising that the Assyrians would not be allowed to enter Jerusalem and that peace would come (2 Ki 19).

4

CAUSES FOR NINEVEH'S DESTRUCTION 3:1-19

God's Indictment Against Nineveh (3:1-4)

Nineveh's notorious violence, falsehood, plunder, ruthlessness, oppression, and cruelty are the direct causes for her downfall (3:1-3). Moreover, she is "the mistress of witchcrafts" who by her sorceries seduced and subjugated nations (3:4), causing even some of the rulers of Israel to subject themselves to her in order to gain her favors. This was true of King Ahaz in 2 Kings 16:7-10.

VERSES 1-3

"Woe to the bloody city" (v.1): The cruelty of the Assyrians, portrayed in verses 1-2, is also well attested by historians. The Assyrians were noted for their ruthlessness and shameful atrocities against other nations. Their victims were mutilated, beheaded, or burned to death. Captured leaders were often flayed and had their skins spread upon the walls of the city. The Assyrian kings boasted of their calculated cruelty in order to instill terror in their enemies. They cut off their limbs or blinded them, while others were impaled on stakes or dragged to death behind chariots. They boasted of the numbers which they had slain and of the captives which they had deported. Cities were razed to the ground, plundered, and burned. The lands were devastated, and the fruit trees destroyed. They exulted in their brutality, bloodshed, and slaughter of their victims. The barbarities which accompanied the capture of a city were incredible, as the excavated inscriptions and sculptures from Assyria attest.

Various modes of execution were employed by the Assyrians. According to George Rawlinson in his writings on the ancient monarchies, impalement on a sharpened stake was a favorite method of execution, doubtless employed by the Assyrians because of its extreme cruelty. A pointed stake was placed in the ground, and the victim was then impaled upon it through his stomach, the stake penetrating inwardly up to his breastbone. Another common mode of executing captives was by crushing the kneeling victim's skull with a mace; others were put to death by beheading them with a sword, or by burning them alive in the fire. Assyrian bas-reliefs from excavated ruins also depict executioners flaying the prisoners with a knife. The victim was tied by his wrists and ankles to stakes in the ground, while the skin was removed from his body with a knife. Mutilation of prisoners was not uncommon with the Assyrians, who cut off their victim's ears, nose, blinded them with hot irons, or plucked out the tongue by the roots.[1]

Inscriptions recovered from Assyrian ruins reveal that Assyrian monarchs delighted in boasting of their cruelties. Writing of one of his conquests, Ashurnasirpal II (883-859 B.C.) boasts:

> I stormed the mountain peaks and took them. In the midst of the mighty mountain I slaughtered them; with their blood I dyed the mountain red like wool. With the

> rest of them I darkened the gullies and precipices of the mountains. I carried off their spoil and their possessions. The heads of their warriors I cut off, and I formed them into a pillar over against their city; their young men and their maidens I burned in the fire. . . . I slaughtered their inhabitants in great numbers, I carried off their spoil, the cities I burned with fire.[2]

Shalmaneser III, describing some of his campaigns, likewise boasted of his cruelties, saying:

> I stormed and captured the city. Multitudes of his warriors I slew. His spoil I carried off. A pyramid of heads I reared in front of his city. Their youths and their maidens I burnt up in the flames.[3]

Describing his treatment of a captured leader, Ashurbanipal said:

> I pierced his chin with my keen hand dagger. Through his jaw I passed a rope, put a dog chain upon him and made him occupy a kennel of the east gate of Nineveh.

Concerning his punishment of other prisoners, his records state:

> I slit their mouths (tongues) and brought them low. The rest of the people, alive . . . I cut down . . . as an offering. Their dismembered bodies I fed to the dogs, swine, wolves, and eagles, to the birds of heaven and the fish of the deep.[4]

The ruthless murder and mutilation of their captives by the Assyrians is all too evident from the following record by Ashurnasirpal:

> With the masses of my troops and by my furious battle

> onset I stormed, I captured the city; 600 of their warriors I put to the sword; 3,000 captives I burned with fire; I did not leave a single one among them alive to serve as a hostage. Hulai, their governor, I captured alive. Their corpses I formed into pillars; their young men and maidens I burned in the fire. Hulai, their governor, I flayed, his skin I spread upon the wall of the city. . . . The city I destroyed, I devastated, I burned with fire.

Concerning another city he continues:

> Many captives from among them I burned with fire, and many I took as living captives. From some I cut off their hands or their fingers, and from others I cut off their noses, their ears, and their fingers; of many I put out their eyes.[5]

"Full of lies": the Assyrians also employed treachery and deceit in extending their conquests, covenanting with national leaders and making them false promises to induce them to submit to their yoke (cf. 2 Ki 18:31-32).

"The noise of the whip" (vv.2-3): Nahum vividly describes here the ruthless conquests of the Assyrian hordes against their enemies: the snap of the whip, the rattling of the wheels, the galloping of the horses, the chariots bounding over the streets, horsemen rearing, the flashing swords and spears, and an endless multitude of corpses, so great that they stumble over the dead. It was her lust for conquest which secured for Nineveh the appellation used by the prophet in verse 1, "the bloody city."

VERSE 4

"The multitude of the whoredoms": the use of the term "whoredoms" actually implies two ideas here. First, it is doubtless a reference to Assyria's harlot-like inducements whereby she allured other nations, so as to subject them to herself, or seduced them by the lure of commerce (cf. 2 Ki 16:7-10; Eze 23:1f.). Second, we find that this term is commonly applied in the Old Testament to idolatry (Ho 1:2; Jer 3:1-2). Certainly idolatry and witchcraft would head the list of crimes for which God intended to judge the Assyrians, as all their bloody conquests were conducted in the name of their gods, and subject nations were required to reverence their deities. The term "whoredoms" is used in this sense in the book of Hosea, for example, where the prophet is commanded by God, "Go, take unto thee a wife of whoredom" (Ho 1:2), in order to illustrate Israel's state of spiritual adultery (idolatry). Because of the bond and covenant relation existing between God and Israel, often represented under the figure of marriage (Ex 34:15; Jer 3:14), the idolatry of Israel was described as whoredom or adultery, and Hosea's marriage to adulterous Gomer was graphically to illustrate this unfaithfulness. Ezekiel also declares that Israel "played the harlot . . . and she doted on her lovers, on the Assyrians her neighbors, who were clothed with blue, governors and rulers, all of them desirable young men, horsemen riding upon horses. And she bestowed her whoredoms upon them . . . with all their idols she defiled herself" (Eze 23:5-7). The term *whoredom* is also applied in Scripture to all apostate religion and idolatry among the nations (2 Ki 9:22; Eze 23:27; Rev 17:1f.).

"The mistress of witchcrafts": as with the Egyptians (Ex 7:11f.) and the Chaldeans (Dan 2), all the heathen nations, including Assyria, employed sorcery and other occult practices in an effort to seduce and overcome others. They sought also by these means to learn their fate, determine the course of the future or outcome of their military campaigns, as well as to gain favor with, or obtain certain powers from, their gods. All such practices were condemned by God without reservation (Deu 18:9-14).

The divine attitude concerning those who participate in the occult, whether nations or individuals, is that of severest rebuke. "For whosoever doeth these things is an abomination unto the Lord" (Deu 18:12). All forms of the occult, such as fortune telling or divination, spiritism, magic practices, and involvement in the false religious cults and their teachings are absolutely forbidden in Scripture, because of the spiritual dangers incurred as a consequence of such involvement.

The teachings of the Old Testament prophets set forth spiritual principles, which by divine intention, are valid for every age. Certainly there has never been a time in history when the warnings against the dangers of occultism were more necessary than the present. The Scriptures warn that there will be such an increase in religious delusion and demonic influence in the last days: "But the Spirit saith expressly, that in later times some shall fall away from the faith, giving heed to seducing spirits and doctrines of demons" (1 Ti 4:1; cf. 2 Th 2:1-11; Mt 24:24).

Reports from all over the world reveal that occultism and witchcraft are rapidly on the increase. Countless millions of dollars are being spent annually on psychic or occult literature, as well as other forms of the occult. Reputable magazines now feature monthly horoscope columns, while millions are being influenced by astrology through the daily newspapers. There is a great upsurge of interest in the black arts with the sales of books on astrology, magic, dreams, ESP, and hypnosis, as well as such occult devices as the ouija board, crystal ball, fortune telling cards, and occult games at an all time record high. Leading sources report that witchcraft is being openly revived all over the world, including the United States. America, England, France, and Germany are finding themselves plagued with the greatest increase in sorcery and occultism since the Middle Ages. Numerous self-admitted witches, warlocks, and devotees of witchcraft now meet regularly to perpetuate rituals and fertility rites, as well as invoke and worship pagan gods (which the Scriptures reveal are demons, Deu 32:16-17; 1 Co 10:20; 1 Ti 4:1).

It is just for this reason that Assyria's sins of witchcraft and sorcery fall under divine judgment. There are, the Scriptures show, two sources of supernatural power and phenomena—God or Satan. Therefore, man is forbidden from seeking information, guidance, or help from occult sources, or from making any contact with them whatsoever, as it is tantamount to calling upon other gods (Ex 20:3-5). Satan is in fact called the "god of this world" (2 Co 4:4), often accommodating the victim with hidden knowledge or some form of help through these occult sources. He deceives the gullible who believe that every miracle, prophecy, revelation, or supernatural event is from God, seemingly unmindful of the fact that Satan can work miracles (Ex 7:11f.; 2 Th 2:9; Rev 13:11-14), inspire false teaching and prophecy (Mt 24:24), or appear as an angel of light (2 Co 11:14).

In the passage in Deuteronomy 18:9-12 we have set forth the methods by which the heathen sought to unveil hidden knowledge, ascertain the future, influence or control events, and invade the spiritual realm by unauthorized means. God warns His people in this passage against participation or involvement in any of these forbidden practices, saying,

> Thou shalt not learn to do after the abomination of those nations. There shall not be found with thee any one . . . that useth divination [fortune telling], one that practiseth augury [astrologer], or an enchanter [magician], or a sorcerer, or a charmer [hypnotist], or a consulter with a familiar spirit [medium possessed with a spirit "guide"], or a wizard [clairvoyant or psychic], or a necromancer [medium who consults the dead]. For whosoever doeth these things is an abomination unto the Lord.

The Scriptures condemn all forms of occultism as sorcery and warn that "they who practice such things shall not inherit the kingdom of God" (Gal 5:19-21), but "is an abomination unto the Lord" (Deu 18:12). From earliest times God forbade witchcraft and all forms of the occult as spiritually defiling (Lev 19:31), and sufficient cause for the rejection of that soul by God (Lev 20:6), making such participation punishable by death (Ex 22:18; Lev 20:27). The seriousness of occult participation is clearly seen in the judgment of God which fell upon King Saul who died by divine decree for seeking help from a medium (1 Sa 28 with 1 Ch 10:13-14).

Further indication of the seriousness of occult involvement in the sight of God is evidenced by the extensive references to the subject in the Scriptures: Exodus 7:11-12 with 2 Timothy 3:8; Exodus 22:18; Leviticus 19:26, 31; 20:6, 27; Deuteronomy 18:9-14; 1 Samuel 15:23; 28; 2 Kings 21:5-6; 1 Chronicles 10:13-14; 2 Chronicles 33:6; Isaiah 2:6; 8:19; Jeremiah 27:9-10; Zechariah 10:2; Malachi 3:5; Acts 8:9f.; 16:16f.; 19:19; Galatians 5:19-21; 1 Timothy 4:1-3; Revelation 21:8; 22:15.[6]

NINEVEH'S DOWNFALL SEALED (3:5-19)

In spite of Nineveh's great power and position, God would soon expose her as a harlot, casting filth upon her, and setting her as a gazing-stock for the nations to see; she will then be forsaken and none will lament her destruction (vv.5-7). She will not be able to avert her overthrow any more than No-amon (Thebes), who, in spite of the waters which had surrounded her like those of Nineveh and the strength of her defenses, was utterly destroyed and the inhabitants carried into captivity (vv.8-11). Her efforts at defense will be futile, the prophet declares; her soldiers will be as weak as women, and although numerous, will be cut off and vanish as locusts who fly away when the sun arises (vv.12-17). Her king and nobles will be slain and the people scattered, amid universal joy among the nations over her downfall (vv.18-19).

VERSES 5-6

The humiliation of Nineveh is described. "I will show the nations thy nakedness, and the kingdoms thy shame. And I will cast abominable filth upon thee . . . and will set thee as a gazing-stock" (vv.5-6). Nineveh is presented here under the figure of a woman who is about to be subjected to the most shameful and disgraceful treatment that could befall her, for God declares, "I will uncover thy skirts upon thy face; I will show the nations thy nakedness" (v.5). Proud Nineveh, as yet unsubdued by the nations, is to be cast down to the ground as a helpless woman and treated as the harlot that she is (3:4). Her glory will be turned into vileness (v.6); and in her humiliation, she will become a gazing-stock before the nations she has oppressed. The same figure is used by Isaiah concerning the downfall of Babylon, who is represented as a virgin woman, not because of her virtue, but as one not yet subdued by others. She too, God declares, is to be cast down, her power and glory removed, and her shame and nakedness exposed to the nations:

> Come down, and sit in the dust, O virgin daughter of Babylon; sit on the ground without a throne, O daughter of the Chaldeans: for thou shalt no more be called tender and delicate [beautiful]. Take the millstones, and grind meal [the master of nations is to be made a servant]; remove thy veil, strip off the train [her glory removed], uncover the leg, [in order to] pass through the rivers [and go into captivity]. Thy nakedness shall be uncovered, yea, thy shame shall be seen (Is 47:1-3).

VERSE 7

"Who will bemoan her?": she who oppressed others will find no comforters in her hour of distress, but will be forsaken and left to her fate. Her oppression and atrocities were so extensive and cruel, and her punishment so richly deserved, that in her own time of need no nation will desire to assist "the bloody city." Nations built upon oppression and wickedness (e.g., Egypt, Assyria, Babylonia, Rome, Nazi Germany) cannot survive, but their power and glory will ultimately be destroyed. In humiliation they shall be made a gazing-stock before the world.

VERSES 8-11

"Art thou better than No-amon?" (v.8): the prophet declares that Nineveh's fate is as certain as that of No-amon in Egypt, who also thought that she was invincible and could not be overthrown. No-amon, located in upper Egypt, was called Thebes by the Greeks and was Egypt's greatest capital at one time.* Thebes was the center of worship of the

* The site today is represented by Luxor and Karnak.

god Amon, from which the Hebrews derived "No-amon," meaning "city of Amon." The Assyrians under Ashurbanipal had destroyed Thebes in 663 B.C. (an event that Nahum looks upon as past), which God uses as an object lesson for the overthrow of Nineveh. Just as Nineveh believed herself invulnerable, being built beside the Tigris River and surrounded by moats (2:8), so too Thebes, located on the Nile and protected by canals, felt secure from her enemies. As Thebes with all her protection was overcome, so too Nineveh, notwithstanding all her fortifications, would be overthrown by her enemies. Moreover, Thebes, unlike Nineveh (3:7), had an abundance of allies in her distress—Ethiopia, Egypt, Put, Lubim (v.9)—and, in spite of all this, she was unable to deliver herself from the enemy (v.10).

"Thou also shall be drunken" (v.11): in their distress and fright they too shall reel and stumble as they flee the enemy (2:5,8,10). "Thou shalt be hid"—that is, "covered over," or "buried"—by God, who will dig her grave (1:14), where she will remain hidden for centuries.

VERSES 12-17

Moreover, Nineveh's defenses will be futile in her day of distress, declares the prophet. "All thy fortresses shall be like fig trees" (v.12): the bloody city's defenses are ready for destruction and will be as readily cast down, and the city devoured by the enemy, as ripe figs fall from the tree when shaken.

"Thy people in the midst of thee are women" (v.13): the warlike Assyrians, the dread of the nations, who were characterized as a lion of prey (2:11-12), will be reduced in strength and in their ability to resist, as women who are helpless against the foe. "The fire hath devoured thy bars": it was the practice of enemy forces, in order to gain access to a fortified city, to build enormous fires against the gates of the city, which devoured both the gates and bars, opening the city wide for invasion. Although Nineveh was laid open and made vulnerable to the enemy as a consequence of the unprecedented flood which destroyed a large portion of her wall (cf. 2:6), the besiegers also attacked her fortifications at various points with fire and other weapons seeking to penetrate the city.

"Draw thee water for the siege" (v.14): the prophet ironically invites the Assyrians to prepare for the siege which is soon to come. "Provide a store of water for the long siege ahead," Nahum bids the inhabitants, "and prepare a supply of bricks in order to repair the breaches in the fortifications when the enemy damages the ramparts," he adds.

"There shall the fire devour thee; the sword shall cut thee off" (v.15): in the very place where they make their preparations for defense the enemy will destroy them, the buildings will be consumed by fire, and the inhabitants slain with the sword. "It shall devour thee like the cankerworm" (a form of locust): the destruction of Nineveh shall be sudden and complete, as that wrought on vegetation by a locust plague. Such a threat had real significance in that part of the world, where devastation by locust hordes is not uncommon yet today. The locust is the most frequently mentioned insect in Scripture, and was one of the ten plagues God inflicted upon Egypt (Ex 10). Because of man's powerlessness to stop them, the locust plague is used in Scripture to symbolize absolute destruction wrought by enemy forces. In the prophecy of Joel, the prophet uses the devastation wrought by a recent locust plague (Joel 1) as a figure to symbolize the destruction to be wrought by invading armies as judgment in the day of the Lord (Joel 2). On the basis of the natural calamity, the people are thus warned and called to repentance. In Near Eastern lands from time to time the locusts begin to multiply in such vast numbers that their swarms extend for miles and are so thick that even the sun cannot penetrate; and when they descend upon the land, they devour all vegetation within reach, even stripping the bark from trees. Such is to be Assyria's fate at the hands of her enemies, Nahum declares.

"Thou hast multiplied thy merchants" (v.16): Nineveh was favorably situated for commerce, located on the trade routes between the east and west, and built beside the Tigris River. She had grown rich not only from her plunder and spoil, but also from her vast trade with other lands. Nevertheless, the enemy, as locusts, would plunder her riches and carry them away, declares the prophet: "the canker-worm ravageth, and fleeth away."

"Thy princes are as the locusts, and thy marshalls as the swarms of grasshoppers" (v.17): in this verse Nahum applies the figure of the locust to the Assyrian leaders themselves; the numbers of their officers were so vast they were compared to the hordes of locusts. "They flee away": cold deprives the locust of its power of flight, but when warmed by the rising sun, it flies away. Nahum by comparison indicates that as the great swarms of locusts disappear as suddenly as they arrive when the sun arises, so the Assyrian leaders will suddenly vanish, having fled the stricken city.[7]

VERSES 18-19

"Thy shepherds slumber" (v.18): perhaps the princes and marshalls of verse 17 are meant here. The prophet gives the explanation for their disappearance—they have fallen asleep; that is, the "sleep" of death (cf. Ps 13:3; 76:6). "O king of Assyria": the reference is to Sinsharishkun, who ruled at the time of Nineveh's downfall.

"There is no assuaging of thy hurt" (v.19): the destruction which Nineveh will undergo is final and completely without remedy. She cannot be restored, for God has declared that He will make her grave and bury her so completely that even her location will become obliterated from history. "All that hear the report of thee clap their hands over thee": the reason is given in conclusion, "for upon whom hath not thy wickedness passed continually?" The cruelty, ruthlessness, and oppression of Nineveh had been universally felt; therefore, all will rejoice in her overthrow. There will be no regret at her downfall; no sympathy will be expressed on her behalf.

Thus, the concluding words of the prophecy reiterate the same theme with which the prophet began: the downfall of Nineveh. The ruthless oppressor shall fall; the "bloody city" will go into oblivion; the ravening lion will be cut off to prey no more. In the judicial punishment of Nineveh is seen the unchanging truth that *righteousness will ultimately triumph, for kingdoms built upon wickedness and tyranny must fall.*

PART TWO
ZEPHANIAH

5

INTRODUCTION TO ZEPHANIAH

The Prophet

The prophet Zephaniah provides no information about himself besides that in the superscription. Here we are informed that he is "the son of Cushi, the son of Gedaliah, the son of Amariah, the son of Hezekiah" (1:1). As it is usually customary for the prophet to name only his father (cf. Jer 1:1; Ho 1:1), it may be inferred that the Hezekiah mentioned is King Hezekiah of Judah (715-686 B.C.). If such is the case, then the prophet would have been a descendant of royalty, as well as a kinsman of King Josiah in whose reign Zephaniah prophesied. Some interpreters have suggested that if this were King Hezekiah he would have been so designated in the genealogy of verse one.[1] However, Zechariah mentions his distinguished ancestor Iddo only by name and not by his office of priest in the superscription of his book (Zec 1:1; cf. Neh 12:4; Ezra 5:1). Moreover, if this is not King Hezekiah in Zephaniah's prophecy, we have no sufficient explanation of the prophet's departing from the customary practice of mentioning only the father in the superscription.

The prophet lived in the southern kingdom of Judah, perhaps in Jerusalem (1:4, 10-11) and was a contemporary of Nahum and Jeremiah. His name means "the Lord hides (protects)," and was borne by three other individuals in the

Old Testament (1 Ch 6:36-38; Jer 21:1; Zec 6:10). Zephaniah's style is direct and assertive due no doubt to the severity of his message of judgment, uttered with impassioned forcefulness against the wicked, not only in Judah, but throughout the world. The book is one prophecy divided into three parts, consisting of a warning of universal judgment, an exhortation to repentance, and the promise of salvation.

Period of Ministry

Zephaniah states that he prophesied "in the days of Josiah" (1:1), who reigned as King of Judah over thirty years (640-609 B.C.). From internal considerations it appears that the prophet conducted his ministry (insofar as his prophecy is concerned) in the early part of Josiah's reign, prior to the king's reformation in 621 B.C. The practices condemned by the prophet in 1:3-6 are precisely those which Josiah abolished by his reforms (cf. 2 Ki 23:4ff.), and the moral and religious conditions described throughout the book seem to indicate that Zephaniah's prophetic activity was instrumental in stirring King Josiah and the people to institute the needed reforms (cf. 2 Ch 34:1-7). Moreover, from the statement in 2:13 it is evident that the destruction of Nineveh in 612 B.C. is an event yet future. From these considerations, a date sometime between 640 and 621 B.C. is suggested for the book.[2]

King Josiah was just a child, eight years of age, when he came to the throne of Judah. The low moral and spiritual conditions resulting from the corrupting influence of the reigns of idolatrous King Manasseh and his son Amon still prevailed in Judah. In the eighth year of Josiah's reign, the king's heart was turned to the Lord; and in the twelfth year, he instituted a program of certain moral and religious reforms, doubtless encouraged by the preaching of Zephaniah (2 Ch 34). Later, in the course of repairing the temple, the high priest found a copy of the book of the law, long neglected under the reigns of Manasseh and Amon, which led to the institution of the great reformation by Josiah in 621 B.C. (2 Ki 22-23).

Purpose of the Prophecy

The theme of the book of Zephaniah, which largely occupies the entire prophecy, is the day of the Lord. The prophecy commences with the announcement of universal judgment, not only upon Judah, but also upon the surrounding nations — the Philistines, the Moabites, Ammonites, Ethiopians, and Assyrians — as well as upon the world in general. Although former prophets had warned of divine judgment awaiting the wicked and disobedient in the day of the Lord (Ob 15; Joel 1:15; Amos 5:18-20; Is 13:6f), Zephaniah's prophecy concentrates upon this theme. It is to be a day when the Lord will make a final intervention in history, destroying the wicked in retributive judgment, and establishing His righteous kingdom. In contrast to the popular misconception in Israel that their election had somehow made them immune from judgment in spite of their idolatry and disobedience, Amos had declared that it was to be for them a day of judgment: "Woe unto you that desire the day of the Lord! Wherefore would ye have the day of the Lord? It is darkness, and not light" (Amos 5:18). Zephaniah takes up the same theme as the earlier prophets, but centers the "day" upon Judah (1:4), as well as the world in general. The dire nature of the day of the Lord is graphically described by the prophet:

> That day is a day of wrath, a day of trouble and distress, a day of wasteness and desolation, a day of darkness and gloominess, a day of clouds and thick darkness. . . . And I will bring distress upon men . . . and their blood shall be poured out as dust, and their flesh as dung. Neither their silver nor their gold shall be able to deliver them in the day of the Lord's wrath; but the whole land [earth] shall be devoured by the fire of his jealousy; for he will make an end, yea, a terrible end, of all them that dwell in the land. (1:15-18).

As righteous Judge, God will sweep away both man and beast in a great world judgment (1:2-3). The day of the Lord is imminent — no one shall escape, even in Jerusalem, for the Lord will search the city with lamps to find the guilty (1:12), and only a remnant will survive (2:3).

Outline of Zephaniah

I. The day of the Lord as judgment, 1:1-3:8
   A. Judgment upon Judah and Jerusalem, 1:1-2:3
      1. The destruction of all things, 1:2-3
      2. The causes of judgment, 1:4-9
      3. The nature of the day of the Lord, 1:10-18
      4. Exhortation to repentance, 2:1-3
   B. Judgment upon the nations, 2:4-15
      1. Judgment against Philistia, 2:4-7
      2. Judgment against Moab and Ammon, 2:8-11
      3. Judgment against Ethiopia, 2:12
      4. Judgment against Assyria, 2:13-15
   C. Announcement of universal judgment, 3:1-8
      1. Woe to Jerusalem, 3:1-7
      2. All nations summoned to judgment, 3:8

II. The day of the Lord as salvation, 3:9-20
   A. Salvation of a remnant among the nations, 3:9-10
   B. The purging and salvation of a remnant in Israel, 3:11-13
   C. The restoration of Israel and establishment of the kingdom, 3:14-20

6

THE DAY OF THE LORD AS JUDGMENT
1:1—3:8

JUDGMENT UPON JUDAH AND JERUSALEM (1:1-2:3)

THE PROPHECY OPENS with an announcement of judgment and destruction upon all things (1:2-3), setting forth the causes for Judah's punishment as apostasy and idolatry (1:4-6), as well as moral and ethical corruption in general (1:7-9). The day of the Lord is characterized as a "sacrifice," in which the victim will be Judah; and the "guests" invited to partake of the offering are the heathen conquerors (1:7). In that day the apostates, who say in their hearts that God will not concern himself with punishing evil or rewarding good, will be searched out and destroyed (1:10-13). The terrible nature of the day is described as a time of "trouble and distress," when nothing shall be able to deliver sinners out of the hand of the Lord (1:14-18). In view of the inevitable destruction coming upon them, the people are urged to repent before the day of the Lord's anger comes upon them (2:1-3).

VERSE 1

"The word of the Lord": the expression applies to the prophecy which follows, as in Micah 1:1 and Hosea 1:1, and is often used in the books of the prophets to refer to a divine revelation from God to the prophet (cf. Jer 1:4 with verse 9; Amos 7:14f.). "In the days of Josiah": about a century before Zephaniah's prophecy, the northern kingdom of Israel had been destroyed by the Assyrians and its inhabitants carried captive. The lesson of God's punishment upon Israel for her sins and idolatry had been wasted upon Judah, who had, by this time, become more corrupt and idolatrous than Samaria (Eze 23). It was in the midst of such wickedness and apostasy that God raised up Zephaniah to warn Judah that a similar fate awaited her as had befallen Israel, unless she repent. Although King Josiah instituted certain moral and religious reforms, Judah's apostasy and corruption were too deeply impressed upon her for any permanent reformation of character, and she too went into captivity when Jerusalem was destroyed by the Babylonians about 35 years later.

VERSES 2-3

"I will utterly consume all things from off the face of the ground, saith the Lord" (v.2): the prophet begins abruptly with an announcement of universal judgment, before he warns Judah of the punishment which awaits her for her sins. The term *ground* in verses 2-3, while directed against Palestine in particular, is not to be limited to judgment upon Judah only, but is to include the entire habitable world. The term is so used in other passages in the Old Testament, as for instance in Amos 3:2, where God says of Israel, "You only have I known of all the families of the earth." The Hebrew term *earth* in this verse is the same as that translated as "ground" in Zephaniah 1:2-3. Again, in Genesis 12:3 this same term is used of the entire world, where God speaking of Abraham promises, "in thee shall all the families of the earth be blessed" (cf. also Gen 28:14; Deu 14:2; Is 24:21). Moreover, in Zephaniah 1:18 the prophet actually uses the term *earth* in the Hebrew (erroneously translated "land" in the KJV and ASV) in reference to the same event to indicate the universality of the judgment on the final day of the Lord. Thus, the term *ground* in verses 2-3 should appropriately be translated "earth," which would be more in harmony with the context of the prophecy.

The scope of divine judgment is clearly to be seen in the graphic statements contained in verses 2-3. "I will utterly consume all things from off the face of the earth . . . man and beast . . . the birds of the heavens, and the fishes of the sea" (vv.2-3a): such language cannot be limited to the little nation of Judah, but is precisely the warning of God given just prior to the flood (Gen 6:7), and thus has reference to the great judgment against all creation in the day of the Lord. "And the stumblingblocks" (v.3): the idols which caused Judah to stumble will also be destroyed, declares the prophet (cf. Eze 14:3-4, 7). Not only will God cut off the wicked because of their idolatry, but He will also sweep away the causes for stumbling, whether actual idols or other incentives to corruption.

VERSES 4-9

Divine judgment is to fall especially upon Judah and Jerusalem, primarily because of their idolatry. "I will cut off the remnant of Baal from this place" (v.4); that is, from Judah and Jerusalem. Sin on the part of those professing to be worshipers of God is always more heinous than that of the world, and is, therefore, judged more severely. Therefore, judgment always begins at the house of God (1 Pe 4:17; cf. Lev 10:1-3; Eze 8-9).

The term *Baal* in Hebrew means "husband," "lord," or "owner," and was also used to designate the god of the Canaanites, whom they believed controlled nature, fertility, and the elements. In their worship of this heathen deity, the Canaanites in Palestine indulged in human sacrifice and licentious rites, as well as other pagan practices. In Israel's transition from the nomadic shepherd to the resident farmer upon her settlement in Palestine, God was aware of the strong attraction that Baalism, a fertility cult, could have upon the nation; hence, His uncompromising decree that the heathen, together with their idolatrous worship, were to be destroyed lest Israel herself become corrupted.

Israel's introduction to Baalism came at the time of the Exodus. Baal worship prevailed among the Moabites and Midianites (Num 22:41), and its infectious attraction spread rapidly among the camp of the Israelites at Baal-peor (Num 25:1-3). The actual worship of Baal was embraced by the Hebrews not long after their entrance into Canaan and is recorded as early as Judges 2:11-14. During the time of Ahab and Jezebel, Baal worship prevailed in the northern kingdom of Israel, as the contest between Elijah and the priests of Baal so clearly indicates (1 Ki 16:30-32; 18:1f.). Baalism was encouraged in the southern kingdom by Jezebel's daughter, Athaliah, who had married Jehoram, King of Judah (2 Ch 21:5-6; 23:1-17). Upon her death, the house of Baal in Jerusalem was destroyed, and its priest slain (2 Ki 11:17-18). There was a revival of Baal worship in Judah during the reign of the wicked King Manasseh (2 Ki 21:1-3), which was put down by Josiah (2 Ki 23) in whose reign Zephaniah prophesied.

The Canaanites had developed a thoroughgoing nature worship which developed out of their agricultural life. The plant cycle was so closely associated with Baal that its various stages were equated with his birth, life, and death, and were celebrated by ritual. At the death of Baal (the decay of vegetation) those who worshiped him wept and tore their hair in grief. At his birth (new growth), festivals of rejoicing were held, the celebrants gathering at the nearest shrine to dance and sing, while indulging in orgiastic ceremonies. Every stretch of fertile ground owed its fertility to Baal. When the Hebrews, a shepherd people, took up agriculture in Canaan, they had practically everything to learn; and it was to their neighbors, the Canaanites, they looked for this education. Quite obviously along with the art of husbandry the Canaanites would transmit the magic and corruption of their religion.

The influence of Baalism among the Hebrews is seen in the fact that over six chapters of 1 Kings is devoted to the reign of Ahab and Jezebel, while scarcely half a chapter is devoted to each of the other kings (with the exception of David and Solomon). Baalism was not just "another religion"; it constituted a serious threat to the worship of God. Under the influence of Ahab and Jezebel, Baalism became the state religion of Israel. No less than 450 prophets of Baal and 400 of Asherah were supported at Jezebel's table, and all dissenters were persecuted and slain. One hundred of the prophets of the Lord were concealed in caves under the supervision of Obadiah (1 Ki 18:3-4). Temples of Baal are mentioned at Samaria and Jerusalem (1 Ki 16:32; 2 Ki 11:18), where they had been erected during the Ahab dynasty. Of all forms of idolatry with which the Israelites came into contact, Baalism was without question the most repugnant to God and perilous to the nation.

The term *Chemarim* concerning Israel's idolatry is probably from a Semitic root meaning "to prostrate oneself" and is always used in the Old Testament to refer to idolatrous priests. Besides this passage in Zephaniah, the term occurs in this sense also in 2 Kings 23:5 and Hosea 10:5. When God declares that He intends to cut off "the name of the Chemarim with the priests" (v.4), He indicates by this that He intends not only to destroy the idol priests but also to eradicate every vestige of such worship.

"And them that worship the host of heaven upon the housetops" (v.5a): the worship of the sun, moon, planets, and stars was an ancient form of idolatry, the heavenly bodies being regarded as deities (Deu 4:15-19). In spite of Moses' warnings, worship of "all the host of heaven" (2 Ki 17:16) is cited as one of the major causes for the downfall of the northern kingdom of Israel, and the idolatrous practice was quite prevalent in Judah in the time of Manasseh as well (2 Ki 21:3).

The flat roofs of their houses, which were used, among other things, as gathering places, were well suited for the worship of the heavenly bodies. Upon these rooftops they erected altars, burned incense, and offered sacrifices (Jer 19:13; 2 Ki 23:12).

Astrology, the ancient practice of divination by consulting the planets and stars, has its roots in this idolatrous worship. Astrologers, star-gazers, and monthly prognosticators are mentioned in Isaiah 47:13, as prevalent in Babylon, which was the source of all apostate religion (Gen 11). This ancient black art is presently undergoing an unprecedented revival, as millions are being influenced by the horoscope columns in the newspapers and magazines. In the United States alone an estimated 5000 astrologers chart the heavens for over 10 million Americans, who plan their lives according to the alleged influence of the heavenly bodies upon human affairs. All forms of occult involvement, including astrology, are condemned by God without reservation in Deuteronomy 18:9-14. (Refer to the exposition on Na 3:4).

"[Them] that swear to the Lord, and swear by Malcam" (v.5b): their worship was a syncretism, that is, an admixture of heathenism and worship of the God of Israel. The term *Malcam* (Malcham) can also mean in Hebrew "their king," but without doubt refers here to the heathen god, Milcom, the Ammonite deity, as it does in Jeremiah 49:3.

Swearing, or the oath, was not forbidden during the Old Testament dispensation, as it is in the New Testament, for a good reason. It was in fact encouraged just as long as the Israelite performed his oath in the name of the Lord. The oath in Israel constituted a religious act. In Moses' exhortations to the people he said: "Thou shalt fear the Lord thy God; and him shalt thou serve, and shalt swear by his name" (Deu 6:13; cf. 10:20; Lev 19:12). Appeal to the name of God instead of the heathen deities constituted a test of loyalty, and was another means by which God sought to wean Israel from her tendency toward idolatry learned in Egypt. However, as Zephaniah indicates, the Israelites had rejected the teaching that God was One (Deu 6:4), and had returned to their former practice of appealing to various deities in performing their oaths, thereby profaning the name of God, as well as the sacredness of the oath in Israel.

In the New Testament, Jesus, referring to God's requirement under the Old Covenant for the Israelites to perform their oaths in legal matters in His name alone, then teaches a higher spiritual principle which the Christian is to follow regarding the oath; namely that of giving a simple answer "yes" or "no" in reply to others (Mt 5:33-37). The same prohibition of the oath is repeated in James 5:12 where we are told: "But above all things, my brethren, swear not, neither by heaven, nor by the earth, nor by any other oath: but let your yea be yea, and your nay, nay; that ye fall not under judgment." All oaths whether judicial, military, or otherwise, were refused by the early Christians, even to the point of death in some instances.[1] The New Testament ethic views any oath as an unnecessary affirmation to the word of a Christian, and, in effect, implies that he may not always tell the truth without it, which is an obvious contradiction to the name he bears.

"Them that are turned back from following the Lord; and those that have not sought the Lord" (v.6). Here the prophet addresses the last two classes of the Israelites who will fall under judicial punishment: the apostates and the spiritually indifferent. Several classes are mentioned in verses 4 to 6 as deserving judgment: the worshipers of Baal, and the Chemarim (v.4); the idolators who worship the heavenly creation (v.5); the syncretists who comingle the worship of the Lord with pagan deities (v.5); and finally, those who have apostatized, or who are guilty of defection in any way, as well as those who despise religion and worship generally (v.6).

"Hold thy peace at the presence of the Lord God" (v.7). Literally, "Be silent!" or "hush!" The admonition is like that in Habakkuk 2:20, the reason for the admonition being the same, "for the day of the Lord is at hand." "For the Lord hath prepared a sacrifice": the "sacrifice" is the guilty Hebrew nation; and his "guests," whom God has invited to partake of the feast, are the Babylonians who will be the divine instrument to carry out His judicial purpose, just as Assyria was in regard to the downfall of the northern kingdom of Israel (Is 10). The figure of the wicked being offered as a "sacrifice" in satisfaction of divine justice is frequent in the prophets (cf. Is 34:6; Jer 46:10; Eze 39:17-19; Rev 19:17-18).

In verses 8-9, the prophet continues the denunciation against other classes who are to fall under divine judgment for their sins. "I will punish the princes, and the king's sons"—that is, both the kings (rulers) and their children—"And all such as are clothed with foreign apparel" (v.8), which implied the adoption by the Israelites of the customs and habits of the foreign nations. Moses had taught that the Israelites were, by sewing tassels and cords of blue upon their garments, to witness that they were a peculiar people, a nation consecrated unto the Lord (Num 15:37-40). The ordinary Israelite unlike the priest did not, of course, wear a religious garb. However, by placing a fringe on the borders of his garment he was to look upon it and remember to obey the commandments of the Lord. To adopt foreign dress would be to dispense with this distinction, as well as to despise its purpose.

"All those that leap over the threshold" (v.9): in all probability this alludes to the priests of the god, Dagon, abstaining from treading on the threshold of their temple in consequence of what took place regarding the overthrow of their idol-god by the Lord at Ashdod (1 Sa 5:1-5). Apparently this pagan custom, among others, was adopted by the superstitious idolators in Israel.* The Philistine custom

* Some suggest that this is a reference to those creditors who crossed over the thresholds of private homes to confiscate something of value as a pledge to insure payment. According to Deuteronomy 24:10-11, he was to stand outside and accept what the debtor offered as security.

arose after the head and hands of their idol (the god Dagon) were cut off on the threshold when it fell before the ark of the Lord. "(Those) that fill their master's house with violence and deceit." Not only the king, and his sons, but also the servants who practice oppression and deceit will be punished. Thus, from the greatest to the least, such offenders will be subjects of God's judicial wrath in the day of the Lord (cf. Is 24:1-6).

VERSES 10-18

The terrible nature of the day of the Lord is described next by the prophet. He introduces this section with the dire announcement that none shall escape, for the Lord will search out the guilty for punishment, their wealth will become a spoil to the enemy, and their houses a desolation.

"And in that day, saith the Lord, there shall be the noise of a cry . . . and a wailing . . . and a great crashing" (v.10): Zephaniah warns the Jews that from various parts of the city, from the fish gate (the gate through which the enemy would enter), from the second quarter (the lower part of the city), and from the hills (the upper part), will come the cry of distress and alarm, when walls and buildings begin to crash down, and the inhabitants are attacked by the enemy forces.

"Maktesh" (v.11), meaning literally "the mortar," refers no doubt to that part of the city situated in a hollow or valley (perhaps to the Tyropoeum Valley at Jerusalem). "The people of Canaan" refers not to the Canaanites themselves but to the Jewish merchants whom God elsewhere derisively calls "Canaanites" because of their greed and deceit in merchandising (cf. Ho 12:7 margin). The term *Canaan* in the Hebrew also means "merchant," because the

Canaanites, especially the Phoenicians, were merchants and traders.

"I will search Jerusalem with lamps" (v.12): the Babylonians, whom God sent against Jerusalem for punishment searched every house and street, even dragging the distressed inhabitants from the sewers and tombs where they had hidden and slaying them. "Settled on their lees": God would search out those who were hardened and unrepentant and consistently ignored the warnings of the prophets of the approaching judgment. The image is taken from the sediment formed by wine left undisturbed for a long period (Jer 48:11; cf. Amos 6:1), a picture of their indifference and spiritually stagnated condition. "That say . . . the Lord will not do good, neither will he do evil": He rebukes those who are agnostic in their attitude toward divine government regarding human affairs. By denying the interest of God in human affairs, the wicked and obdurate attempt to excuse their conduct. They want to live as they please, as if God were unconcerned about their morality; hence, they deny His judicial concern, thinking thereby that they have also dispensed with His judicial punishment of wrongdoers (cf. Ps 10:4; 14:1; 73:11).

"Their wealth shall become a spoil, and their houses a desolation" (v.13): their temporal possessions which consumed their time and interests, while they despised spiritual values, will become plunder for the enemy, as they will not live to enjoy them (thus fulfilling the curse of the law, Deu 28:30; cf. Amos 5:11).

"The great day of the Lord is near" (v.14): this is the theme of Zephaniah's prophecy. The concept appears in the preaching of all the prophets and is sometimes spoken of as "that day" (Mic 2:4; Ho 5:9). Isaiah makes use of both expressions (Is 2:12; 3:7). Jeremiah declared that it was to be a day of divine judgment upon sin and disobedience (Jer 25:33; 46:10). On the basis of her election, Israel thought herself immune from punishment in spite of her sins, and looked with expectation for the day of the Lord to come. Amos, however, corrects the popular conception, declaring that it is to be a day of darkness and not light (Amos 5:18-20).

This day was to fall not only upon the disobedient nation of Israel, but would bring universal judgment upon all nations. Amos arraigns Israel's neighbors before the throne of judgment (Amos 1:3-2:3). Isaiah announces judgment upon Philistia (Is 14:28-32), and Damascus (Is 17:1f); Egypt and Ethiopia will be cut down (Is 20:1-6; 31:1-5); and Babylon will be overthrown in the day of the Lord (Is 13:1f). Jeremiah 46:10 and Ezekiel 30 both foretell Egypt's downfall in the day of the Lord. Isaiah 24:1-7 depicts the universal judgment of the entire world in that day as do Joel 3:1-16, Zechariah 12-14, and Obadiah 15. Through Zephaniah God declares: "I will utterly consume all things from off the face of the [earth] . . . man and beast . . . birds . . . and the fishes. . . . I will cut off man from off the face of the ground [earth], saith the Lord" (1:2-3).

The day of the Lord is not to be limited to one day, or a single instance of divine judgment, but encompasses every instance when judgment has fallen upon nations in fulfillment of prophecy concerning them. Ultimate fulfillment of the prophecies of universal judgment, however, is reserved until the great and final day of the Lord at Christ's return.

"The voice of the day of the Lord" (v.14): Amos also speaks of the sound of the Lord's voice in that day as like the roar of a lion (Amos 1:2), as do Jeremiah 25:30, and Joel 3:16. "The mighty men crieth there bitterly," for in that day even the brave warrior and fearless leader will be panic stricken with fear before the wrath of the Lord (cf. Rev. 6:12-17).

Zephaniah warns, "That day is a day of wrath" (v.15), and follows this announcement with a vivid description of the terrible nature of the day. "A day of trouble and distress": it will be a time of extreme affliction and anxiety, without hope of assistance or deliverance. "A day of wasteness and desolation": precisely the picture that Isaiah depicts when the earth is made waste and is in a state of utter desolation as a consequence of divine judgment (Is 24:1f.). Zephaniah also adds that it will be "a day of darkness and gloominess, a day of clouds and thick darkness."

Moreover, it is to be "a day of trumpet and alarm" (v.16), signifying the sounding of alarm, which was the custom at the approach of an enemy (cf. Jer 4:5; Eze 33:4).

"They shall walk like blind men" (v. 17), as a result of their distress. In their anxiety and helplessness they will grope about, wandering aimlessly as blind men in a state of shock. However, this is not to be limited to a mere figurative judgment upon the wicked; but God also declares that the disobedient would be smitten with a plague and curse, resulting in actual blindness, which would increase their terror and distress (Deu 28:28-29; Zec 14:12-15). "Their blood shall be poured out as dust, and their flesh as dung," thereby indicating the abundance of the slaughter in the day of the Lord.

"Neither their silver nor their gold shall be able to deliver them" (v.18): men have often been able to purchase for themselves immunity from the threats of an enemy (cf. 2 Ki 18:13f.), but Zephaniah declares that the guilty will not be able to bribe this One who comes in judgment (cf. Is 13:17). Ezekiel foretold how the wicked, in the day of the Lord, in their utter terror will "cast their silver in the streets, and their gold shall be as an unclean thing; their silver and their gold shall not be able to deliver them in the day of wrath of the Lord" (Eze 7:19). "The whole land [earth] shall be devoured by the fire of his jealousy" is precisely the nature of judgment predicted in the New Testament, which is to befall the whole earth in the day of the Lord (2 Pe 3:10-13).

CHAPTER 2, VERSES 1-3

In view of the inevitable destruction coming upon the earth, the prophet urges all to repent, especially praying for the meek and faithful to seek the Lord more earnestly than ever to insure their own preservation from wrath in the terrible day of the Lord.

"Gather yourselves together" (v.1): the people are called to convene an assembly for the purpose of seeking the mercy of the Lord in humble repentance (cf. Joel 2: 15-17). "Before the decree [to punish the wicked] bring forth" (v.2): the threat is repeated three times to enforce the certainty of judgment. "Seek ye the Lord, all ye meek of the earth. . . . it may be ye will be hid in the day of the Lord's anger" (v.3): this does not imply doubt as to the deliverance of the righteous, but that it is not to be taken for granted, lest, as some, they grow careless. It is an exhortation to continued faithfulness (1 Pe 4:17-19; Is 26: 20-21; Mt 5:5).

Thus, before resuming his message of judgment against the nations, the prophet entreats estranged Judah to consider her ways and repent before it is too late. Such is the condescending grace of the Lord. He might have left them to suffer the consequences of their sins; nevertheless, as in every age, God's love first seeks restoration of the erring transgressor before judgment comes. But there must be no delay, the prophet cautions them, as the day of the Lord is at hand, thus echoing the prophetic warning heard throughout the Scriptures: "Seek ye the Lord while he may be found; call ye upon him while he is near" (Is 55:6); "behold, now is the acceptable time; behold, now is the day of salvation" (2 Co 6:2).

JUDGMENT UPON THE NATIONS (2:4-15)

The day of the Lord will not only engulf Judah, but also Philistia, who will be destroyed, their land being given to the remnant of Judah for grazing their flocks and herds when the Lord restores His people (2:4-7). Moab and Ammon will also be punished, the former becoming as Sodom, and the latter as Gomorrah (2:8-10). Upon the destruction of the wicked among the nations, the surviving "men shall worship him, every one from his place, even all the isles of the nations" (2:11), at which time the Lord will be universally recognized. Ethiopia will not escape judgment, but will be cut down by the sword (2:12); the Lord will also stretch forth His hand and "destroy Assyria, and will make Nineveh a desolation" (2:13-15). The judgment threatened against Judah and upon the nations mentioned by Zephaniah is to be a forerunner of universal judgment which will befall the whole world in the great day of the Lord (1:2-3; 3:8).

VERSES 4-7

"For Gaza shall be forsaken, and Ashkelon a desolation;

they shall drive out Ashdod at noonday, and Ekron shall be rooted up" (v.4): the prophet announces judgment upon four of the five cities of the Philistines, Gath being at this time under Jewish control (1 Ch 18:1). When God sends the invading armies of the Babylonians against Judah they will also destroy the powerful Philistines which surround her, thus providing additional incentive for Judah to repent while there is still time. As in Micah 1:10-15, the prophet employs the use of paronomasia (a play on words) in the Hebrew to add emphasis to his foreboding announcement.[2]

The names of these cities become symbolic and prophetic of the nature of their punishment. The meaning and sometimes the sound of their names in Hebrew becomes the basis for the prophet's play on words, which is lost in the English translation. It is as if the prophet had said, "Flint (Michigan) shall be broken"; "Great Falls shall fall by the sword"; or "Pittsburgh shall be cast into the pit"; and so on.

"Gaza shall be forsaken": in the Hebrew there is a play both upon sound—*Azzāh* shall be *Azûbāh*—as well as sense. The Hebrew term *Gaza* (*Azzāh*) means "strong" or "mighty," while *Azûbāh* signifies "forsaken" or "desolation." The prophet thus indicates by the use of the latter term that the "strong" and "mighty" city would be overcome, and that she would be "forsaken" and "deserted." "Ashkelon a desolation": if its name is derived from the escallot (scallion) which grew abundantly there as some suppose,[3] then the prophet intended a play upon that meaning; namely, the site which was noted for its fertility shall become a desolation. Moreover, Ashkelon, located as it was on the Mediterranean Sea, was noted for its commerce and lucrative trade; nevertheless, she was to become barren and desolate in contrast to her present prosperity. "They shall drive out Ashdod at noonday." The paronomasia here stems from the meaning of the term *Ashdod,* which signifies in the Hebrew "stronghold" or "fortress." The stronghold of the Philistines, a fortress in strength, would become so defenseless that there will be no need for a surprise attack after dark by the enemy forces, but she can be overthrown at noon, in broad daylight. An attack at noon implies contempt for Ashdod's reputation as a formidable city. "Ekron shall be rooted up": in the Hebrew *Ekron* means "to root up," the play upon meaning being obvious in this instance.

"Woe unto the inhabitants of the sea-coast, the nation of the Cherethites" (v.5). The LXX (Septuagint) renders the term *Cherethites* as Cretans, inasmuch as the Philistines originally came to Palestine from Crete (Caphtor, Amos 9:7;** cf. 1 Sam 30:14; Eze 25:16.

"The sea-coast shall be pastures" (v.6). The region shall be so depopulated that it will be transformed from an urban area to pasturage for nomadic shepherds and flocks.

"And the coast shall be for the remnant of the house of Judah . . . for the Lord their God will visit them, and bring back their captivity" (v.7): the promise has a twofold fulfillment: first, in their return from exile in Babylon in 536 B.C.; second, in the latter days during the millennium. Contrary to the view of some interpreters, the national restoration of Israel is promised again and again in Scripture, and is discussed in the exposition of chapter 3 where the promise is repeated in verse 20.

The prophetic doctrine of the deliverance of a remnant does not have its origin with Zephaniah, but had been

** Perhaps Caphtor included Crete in the Mediterranean as well as other islands in the vicinity.

enunciated by the earlier prophets. Obadiah in the ninth century foretold of those who would "escape" in the day of the Lord and would "possess their possessions" (Ob 17). The prophet Joel also proclaimed this in the same century (Joel 2:32-3:1ff.). Amos in the eighth century stressed the fact that a righteous remnant would be preserved in the day of the Lord, having survived God's sifting of the Hebrews among the nations (Amos 5:15; 9:11f.); while Isaiah deals extensively with the restoration of the righteous remnant. Even his son had been given the symbolic name, Shearjashub, meaning "a remnant shall return" (Is 7:3), a divine promise of their restoration from Babylon (cf. Is 10:20-22; 37:32).

The roots of the remnant doctrine are to be found in God's revelation to Elijah, when the prophet despairing for his life and believing himself to be the last of those remaining faithful to the Lord, was told that God had preserved for Himself 7,000 in Israel who had not forsaken Him and worshiped Baal (1 Ki 19:18). Jeremiah adds new significance to the remnant concept in his teaching on the new covenant which God will make with His people (Jer 31:31-33), as does Ezekiel, who also conceives of a regenerate and faithful remnant to whom God has given a "new heart" (Eze 36:26-27). The remnant hope is also found in Micah, where the remnant will constitute a people over whom the Lord will reign (Mic 4:6-7). In Daniel it is the saints of the Most High who are to be preserved in order to possess the kingdom (Dan 7:21-27), while Zechariah depicts a remnant being preserved in Zion in the day of the Lord (Zec 14:1f.). The last prophet of the Old Testament dispensation concludes his prophecy concerning the judgment to befall the earth in the day of the

Lord with the promise that those who are faithful and fear the name of the Lord will not perish with the wicked on that day (Mal 4:1-3). The doctrine is taken up and enlarged upon by Christ and the apostles in the New Testament (e.g., Mt 7:21-22; 13:1ff.; Ro 9, 11; Rev 7).

VERSES 8-11

"I have heard the reproach of Moab, and the revilings of . . . Ammon" (v.8): turning now from the Philistines, the prophet addresses Moab and Ammon. These two nations, descendants of Lot, proved themselves bitter enemies of the Hebrews. God charges them with reviling and reproaching His people, and with violating Israel's border and territorial rights (v.8b), in addition to pride (v.10). Pride and arrogancy were characteristic of these two nations according to the prophets (cf. Is 16:6; Jer 48:29; Eze 25:1-7). Although disobedient Judah herself is guilty and deserving of punishment, nevertheless, on the basis of the principle set forth in Genesis 12:3 ("I will bless them that bless thee, and him that curseth thee will I curse"), judgment is often pronounced in the Old Testament upon the persecutors and revilers of God's chosen nation, Israel. Moreover, the offense of Moab and Ammon is increased in God's sight because of their kinship to the Hebrews through Abraham and Lot.

"Moab shall be as Sodom, and . . . Ammon as Gomorrah" (v.9): this threat would have special significance to Moab and Ammon whose territory was located in the Dead Sea region, and because their ancestor, Lot, was closely involved in the destruction of those two wicked cities (Gen 18-19). The threat here is of complete destruction, their fertile land becoming desolate, a place for nettles and salt pits. This is what they will reap because of their pride (v.10).

"He will famish all the gods of the earth" (v.11): the meaning here seems to be that one day worshipers will no longer be found to offer sacrifices unto the heathen gods, who will, from lack of devotees, pass away. The reason is given in the next clause: "men shall worship him [the Lord], every one from his place, even all the isles of the nations." In the day of the Lord idolatry will be abolished, and the true God of Israel will be universally acknowledged and worshiped (cf. 3:9; Zec 14:9; Mal 1:11; Jn 4:21-24). "*From his place*" is taken by some to mean not merely universal worship but that the Gentiles will one day come *from* their different *places* to worship God at Jerusalem during the millennium on the basis of such passages as Isaiah 2:2; Micah 4:1-2; and Zechariah 8:22; 14:16. Certainly both meanings may be intended here—universal worship as well as direct worship of the Lord at Jerusalem, when He returns to reign in Zion as the Scriptures quite frequently attest (Is 2:1-4; 14:1-2; 49:22-23; 60:1-14; 66:18-21, 23; Mic 4:1-4; Zec 2:10-12; 8:20-23; 14:9, 16f.; Zep 3:10, margin; Rev 7; 20:4-9).

VERSES 12-15

Ethiopia and Assyria are denounced next in the prophecy. "Ye Ethiopians also, ye shall be slain by my sword" (v.12): this prediction was fulfilled when God sent Babylon against Ethiopia and its closely connected ally, Egypt (Eze 30:4-9; 2 Ki 24:7). Later the Persian, Greek, and Roman empires successively dominated their land. "*My sword*" designates Babylon. See Isaiah 10:5-6 where God in the same manner designated Assyria as His rod of punishment against Israel.

"He will stretch out his hand against the north, and destroy Assyria, and will make Nineveh a desolation" (v.13): this is precisely the fate foretold by Zephaniah's contemporary Nahum for the wicked nation and its capital Nineveh, this being the theme of the latter's prophecy.

"And herds shall lie down in the midst of her, all the beasts of the nations [the earth]" (v.14): where there was once a teeming population, there shall be such desolation that the area shall become a habitation for the wild birds and beasts.

"This is the joyous city that dwelt carelessly" (v.15): proud and secure because of her great power and defenses, Nineveh carelessly believed herself invulnerable. Thus she boasted: "I am, and there is none besides me." Assyrian conquests had enabled her to dominate the Near Eastern world, and the nation was at this time at the height of its glory and prosperity under Ashurbanipal (669-633 B.C.). Such boasts seem to be the popular form of expression by the great monarchs of ancient history, as Isaiah also records just such an expression of pride made by Babylon (Is 47:8). Such is generally the spirit of the world powers, ancient and modern, who, trusting in their strength of arms and defenses, boast: "I am, and there is none else besides me" (Is 47:10). Not only will God bring such nations to desolation and ruin, but will also make them a derision before the other nations of the world, so that "everyone that passeth by her shall hiss, and wag his hand [in contempt]."

Announcement of Universal Judgment (3:1-8)

From Nineveh the prophet turns again to Jerusalem and contrasts her sinfulness with God's righteousness. Jerusalem has been rebellious, oppressive, and faithless (3:1-2). Especially to be rebuked are her leaders: her princes and judges are motivated only by greed; her prophets are unreliable and treacherous; and the priests are unholy, and are unfaithful to the requirements of the law (3:3-4). The Lord, in contrast, is righteous, giving evidence daily of His justice. He has cut off wicked nations (including Israel) as a warning to Judah, intending that they should profit thereby and repent; but, on the contrary, "they rose early and corrupted all their doings" (3:5-7). Therefore, Judah, along with the nations, will be reserved for punishment in the day of the Lord (3:8).

VERSES 1-2

"The oppressing city" (v.1). Jerusalem is addressed here, as the context which follows indicates (vv.2-7). She is charged with numerous sins: she is "rebellious," morally "polluted," and guilty of the oppression of the poor, widows, and orphans (cf. Jer 22:3).

"She obeyed not the voice" (v.2): this was the voice of the law and the prophets. "She received not correction": thus she ignored her past lessons of discipline and chastisement (Jer 5:3). "She trusted not in the Lord": she trusted instead in her own wisdom and in her foreign alliances when threatened by the enemy. "She drew not near to her God," in worship and faithful service; but, according to 1:4-6, she worshiped Baal and the hosts of heaven (3:2).

VERSES 3-4

"Her princes . . . are roaring lions" (v.3): her rulers devour the people and their substance as lions of prey (cf. 2 Ki 21:16; Mic 3:1-3). "Her judges are evening wolves; they leave nothing till the morrow": those whose duty it was to administer equity and justice are themselves the most greedy and rapacious. Because of their avariciousness, they devour their victims immediately and so completely that there is nothing left. Ezekiel rebukes them: "Her princes . . . are like wolves ravening the prey, to shed blood, and to destroy souls, that they may get dishonest gain" (Eze 22:27).

"Her prophets are light and treacherous persons" (v.4): these are the prophets who speak out of their own heart and not by the Spirit of the Lord. They are "light," charges Zephaniah, meaning that their utterances are shallow and superficial; but they are at the same time "treacherous," indicating that their intention is to deceive, as well as pretend that their message is from the Lord. They prophesy for hire, and deceive the gullible out of their possessions, according to Ezekiel 22:25. During the same period, Jeremiah also rebuked and denounced the deceitful prophets, charging them with speaking "a vision of their own heart, and not out of the mouth of the Lord" (Jer 23:16).

"Her priests have profaned the sanctuary, they have done violence to the law": the prophet Ezekiel describes this desecration of the sanctuary: "Her priests . . . have profaned my holy things; they have made no distinction between the holy and the common, neither have they caused men to discern between the unclean and the clean, and have hid their eyes from my sabbaths, and I am profaned among them" (Eze 22:26). They had not respected that which was consecrated to God as holy, treating it as common; they had ignored the separation between the clean and unclean in total disregard to the religious distinctions God ordained His priests to observe (Lev 10:10); and they had sanctioned violations of the holy days and, in teaching the people to do so, had done violence to the law.

VERSES 5-7

In contrast to Judah's sinfulness and the people's unfaithfulness to Him, God reminds them of His righteousness and lovingkindness toward them.

"Every morning doth he bring his justice to light" (v.5): He did this by means of the preaching of the prophets and through the teaching of the law by the faithful priests. God reiterated this same truth through His prophet Jeremiah: "Since the day that your fathers came forth out of the land of Egypt until this day, I have sent unto you all my servants the prophets, daily rising up early and sending them: yet they hearkened not unto me, nor inclined their ear" (Jer 7:25-26). God had not left Himself without a witness as to His requirements, nor to His love and concern for them; thus, it is not from ignorance that the people have sinned and been unfaithful to Him.

"I have cut off nations . . . so that none passeth by" (v.6): true to His promise, God had destroyed their enemies in Palestine. Under David He had subdued the surrounding nations as well, thus leaving them free and undisturbed from the threat of invasion so that they could develop their land and in peace worship God.

"I said, Only fear thou me; receive correction" (v.7): His gracious purpose in their former discipline and correction was to awaken them to their moral and religious transgressions, and turn them back to loving obedience. However, His warnings and correction were in vain; they could not wait until the next day to resume their life of dissipation and sin, for "they rose up early and corrupted all their doings."

VERSE 8

Because of this, the Lord warns Judah: "Therefore, wait ye for me . . . until the day that I rise up to the prey" (v.8). Because of her favored position with the Lord, and on the basis of the divine promises made to her, Judah had come to look upon herself as immune from such destruction as befell the apostate northern kingdom of Israel, especially since she had now survived for over a century after its downfall. The supernatural overthrow of the mighty Assyrian host under Sennacherib in the time of Hezekiah, as well as Judah's present prosperity, had only heightened this illusion. But the divine judicial principle set forth here (cf. 2 Pe 3:8-10) is that delay in punishment of the guilty does not imply that it has been overlooked or set aside. Thus, the Lord disdainfully informs the rebellious and indifferent Jews, "Wait ye for me . . . until the day"; that is, the day of the Lord, which is the central theme of Zephaniah's prophecy. "For my determination [decree] is to gather the nations . . . to pour upon them mine indignation . . . for all the earth shall be devoured with the fire of my jealousy": a repetition of the announcement of universal judgment as found in Joel 3:1-2; Zechariah 14:1-3; and Matthew 25:31-33. The phrase "fire of my jealousy" is a reference to the destruction of all things by fire because of the divine jealousy aroused as a consequence of man's unfaithfulness in turning from the true God, who had created and blessed him with many graces, to the allurements offered by the god of this world, Satan.

7

THE DAY OF THE LORD AS SALVATION
3:9-20

SALVATION OF A REMNANT AMONG THE NATIONS (3:9-10)

WHEN DIVINE JUDGMENT has accomplished its work, then God will gather the remnant of people from the nations who will worship him in purity and holiness, and with one consent.

VERSE 9

"For then will I turn [restore] to the peoples a pure language, that they may all call upon the name of the Lord" (v.9): the Gentiles' lips had been rendered impure, being used to call upon their idols. God promises that He will purify their lips, which have been polluted with the names of false gods in their worship of them, through the restoration of the worship of the name of the one true God (cf. Ps 16:4; Ho 2:17). Although this promise may have some application to Messianic times at the first advent, its primary reference is to the age of the millennium when God destroys those antagonistic to Him and turns the remnant from all nations unto Him in the day of the Lord. Then they shall all speak the same language of faith in God, serving Him with one consent.

The Hebrew term translated "turn" has the sense here of "restore." As a penalty for their rebellion at Babel (Gen. 11), God sent a confusion of language in order to disrupt their plans. The day is to come when there will be a restoration of the earth's unity of language and worship. The curse of Babel which has divided and scattered the peoples will be removed. The outpouring of the Holy Spirit at Pentecost was an earnest of the removal of this penalty, as Jews from all over the world heard without need of an interpreter the disciples speaking in their various languages about the mighty works of God, as the Spirit gave them utterance (Ac 2:4).

The prophet Joel spoke of this time of the restoration of a pure language in the latter days: "I will pour out my Spirit upon all flesh; and your sons and your daughters shall prophesy" (Joel 2:28). From Peter's words on the day of Pentecost, he indicated that this promise was not limited to Pentecost, but was to have continuous fulfillment from that day unto eschatological times.[1] The apostle does not say, as some have suggested, that Pentecost fulfilled this promise.[2] In reply to the Jew's question, "What meaneth this?" he answered, "This is that which hath been spoken through the prophet Joel" (Ac 2:12, 16), cautiously omitting the use of the term *fulfillment.* On the contrary, he clearly states that the promise extends unto eschatological times, saying, "For to you is the promise, and to your children, and to all that are afar off, even as many as the Lord our God shall call unto him" (Ac 2:39). From this we see that the promise was not "fulfilled" at Pentecost; nor, as Gaebelien suggests, is its application to be limited only to Israel when she is restored in the latter days.[3] However, the full restoration of the earth's unity of language and worship when all alike are filled with the Spirit of prophecy and praise is yet future and is connected, as the following verses in Zephaniah show, with the restoration of Israel (cf. Is 19:18; Zec 14:1-9).

VERSE 10

"From beyond the rivers of Ethiopia my suppliants, even the daughter of my dispersed, shall bring mine offering" (v.10): the phrase "the daughter of my dispersed" is a Hebrew idiom meaning "my dispersed people"; that is, the Jews scattered among the nations of the world. Here they are made the representative of all the Jews who will be ultimately restored, inasmuch as "beyond the rivers of Ethiopia" is to be taken to mean "from the remotest parts of the earth." Ethiopia (Cush) was the southern extremity of the known world at that time, which also appears to be the southern terminus of the judgments in 2:12.[4]

In view of the teaching elsewhere in Scripture, it is better to render the verse as the ASV margin indicates, which is the correct rendering of the Hebrew: "They shall bring my suppliants, even the daughter of my dispersed, for an offering unto me." That is to say, the Gentiles, when they have been turned to the Lord (2:11; 3:9), will then show their faith and love by aiding the Jews among their nations to turn to Christ. This shall then constitute an offering unto the Lord. Isaiah likewise foretold of this time: "I will gather all nations and tongues; and they shall come, and shall see my glory. . . . And they shall bring all your brethren out of all the nations for an oblation [offering] unto the Lord . . . to my holy mountain Jerusalem" (Is 66:18, 20). The apostle Paul without question also has this concept in mind in his teaching concerning Israel and the church in Romans 11. In Isaiah 49:22, God promises Israel, "Behold, I will lift up my hand to the nations . . . and they shall bring thy sons in their bosom, and thy daughters shall be carried upon their shoulders." Compare also Isaiah 14:1-2; 43:5-6; and 60:9.

This prophecy will find particular fulfillment now at the close of the age. This is to be seen, for example, in the aid which some Gentile nations have given to Israel, including the prayers of Christians, in her national restoration to her land which is preparatory to her spiritual restoration in Christ (Ro 11). Moreover on the basis of Scripture it is not improbable to suppose that the time will come when, because of the abundance of God's blessings upon the nation of Israel and His evident presence among them, that many nations and their leaders will strive to obtain God's favor also by their help and concern for the Jews. This is precisely what is foretold by the prophets. In Zechariah 8:22-23, God declares: "Yea, many peoples and strong nations shall come to seek the Lord of hosts in Jerusalem, and to entreat the favor of the Lord. Thus saith the Lord of hosts: In those days it shall come to pass, that ten men shall take hold, out of all the languages of the nations, they shall take hold of the skirt of him that is a Jew, saying, We will go with you, for we have heard that God is with you." In addition to the passages already cited, note also: Genesis 12:3; Isaiah 49:22-23; 60:1-14; Zephaniah 3:19-20.

The Purging and Salvation of a Remnant in Israel (3:11-13)

In that day the proud and rebellious will be purged out of Israel, leaving an "afflicted and poor people," which will constitute the remnant of Israel, who will then trust in the Lord.

VERSE 11

"In that day shalt thou not be put to shame for all thy doings" (v.11): after Israel is purged of the proud and rebellious, she will no longer have to reproach herself for her sinful past and unfaithfulness, for her sins will be blotted out forever. In Ezekiel 20:33-38, God speaks of this day when He will gather all Israel before Him in judgment and purge out the rebels from the remnant of the faithful.

> As I live, saith the Lord God, surely with a mighty hand, and with an outstretched arm, and with wrath poured out, will I be king over you. And I will bring you out from the peoples, and will gather you out of the countries wherein ye are scattered, with a mighty hand, and with an outstretched arm, and with wrath poured out; and I will bring you into the wilderness of the peoples, and there will I enter into judgment with you face to face. . . . And I will cause you to pass under the rod, and I will bring you into the bond of the covenant; and I will purge out from among you the rebels, and them that transgress against me; I will bring them forth out of the land where they sojourn, but they shall not enter into the land of Israel.

VERSES 12-13

"But I will leave in the midst of thee an afflicted and poor people" (v.12): they will not be afflicted and poor in the sense of being diseased and poverty-stricken, but God speaks of their changed attitude and character as a result of their purging. In that day the followers of the Lord will be contrite and humble in spirit, no longer proud and self-assured.

"The remnant of Israel shall not do iniquity, nor speak lies; neither shall a deceitful tongue be found in their mouth" (v.13): both their conduct and character will be changed. The final clause in this verse is based upon the imagery of Psalm 23: "they shall feed and lie down, and none shall make them afraid." The cleansed remnant is compared to a flock of lambs of whom the Lord is Shepherd.

The Restoration of Israel and Establishment of the Kingdom (3:14-20)

When the Lord shall take away her judgments, He will restore His nation and, as King, reign in her midst. Establishing His millennial kingdom on the earth, He will deal with those who have afflicted His people, and make her name a praise through the earth, instead of a reproach.

VERSES 14-18

"Sing, O daughter of Zion" (v.14): the prophet gives the reasons for her rejoicing in the verses which follow.

"The Lord hath taken away thy judgments" (v.15): this is the first cause for rejoicing. The Lord hath taken away her chastisements, which were the result of her disobedience. When the cause (her sin) has been removed, then the effect (freedom from judgment) follows.

"He hath cast out thine enemy" (v.15): the Babylonians were her great threat and God's instruments of judgment (cf. Habakkuk); however, the reference speaks of the final overthrow of Israel's enemies in the latter days (3:19).

"The King of Israel, even the Lord, is in the midst of thee (v.15): clearly this refers to the restoration of the theocracy during the millennium with Christ, as King, reigning in the midst of Israel—a fact which is reiterated again and again in Scripture.

Old Testament references concerning Israel's restoration also speak of the restoration of the city of Zion as her possession, which is to be the dwelling place of the glorified Messiah and the seat of His theocratic government during the millennial reign of Christ (e.g., Is 2:1-3; Mic 4:1-2; Zec 2:1-12; 8:1f; 14:1-21; Eze 40-48). This is confirmed in the New Testament, for example, in Jesus' teaching in Luke 21:24, saying, "Jerusalem shall be trodden down of the Gentiles, until the times of the Gentiles be fulfilled." In fulfillment of this prophecy, Israel, who had been dispossessed of her city for nineteen centuries, had her holy city restored to her in 1967 as the Scriptures predicted. Of course, this is preparatory, as was Israel's restoration as a nation in 1948, to her ultimate spiritual restoration at the return of Christ to reign in Zion (Rev 19-20).

"Thou shalt not fear evil any more" (v.15): they shall no longer experience adversity.

"In that day it shall be said to Jerusalem, Fear thou not; O Zion, let not thy hands be slack (v.16): that is, "Take courage! for your judgments are now past, your enemies are destroyed, and the Lord now dwells in your midst once more."

"The Lord thy God is in the midst of thee, a mighty one who will save; he will rejoice over thee with joy; he will rest in his love; he will joy over thee with singing (v.17): clearly a reference to the future, it was evidently unfulfilled at the first advent when Christ lamented over Israel's rejection of Him, saying,

> O Jerusalem, Jerusalem, that killeth the prophets, and stoneth them that are sent unto her! how often would I have gathered thy children together, even as a hen gathereth her chickens under her wings, and ye would not! Behold, your house is left unto you desolate. For I say unto you, Ye shall not see me henceforth, till ye shall

> **say, Blessed is he that cometh in the name of the Lord. (Mt 23:37-38).**

John also said in this regard, "He came unto his own, and they that were his own received him not" (Jn 1:11). "He will rest [Heb. "be silent"] in his love": this silence arises from the fact that He no longer has anything to rebuke or denounce them for (cf. 3:8).

"I will gather them that sorrow for the solemn assembly" (v.18): the pious Israelites, because of their exile from their land and temple, had been unable to worship their God with proper observance of the feasts, offerings, and the holy days (cf. Lam 1:4; 2:6-7). This is to be restored (with modifications), and the Lord encourages the pious Israelite to rejoice in this promise. In Ezekiel 40:1-46:24, there is a clear and detailed prophecy concerning the reestablishment of the temple and worship for Israel, reconstituted and modified, of course, during the millennium.[5] "The burden upon her was a reproach." Their exile and dispossession was a reproach which she carried as a burden.

VERSE 19

"Behold, at that time I will deal with all them that afflict thee" (v.9): the restoration of Israel is accompanied by the destruction of her oppressors. As pointed out in 2:8, on the basis of the principle given in Genesis 12:3 ("I will bless them that bless thee, and him that curseth thee will I curse"), judgment is pronounced by God upon all who persecute or afflict His chosen people, Israel.

The Scriptures declare that Israel is God's first love to whom He inseparably wed Himself in the wilderness as her Husband (Jer 3:14); and although He may chasten her for her unfaithfulness, He will not cast her off forever but will restore their relationship as Husband and wife once more (Ho 2:14-20). She is called by Him "the apple of His eye" (Deu 32:10; Zec 2:8); and even while she is scattered and being chastened, God jealously watches over the conduct of other nations toward her. The Scriptures repeatedly warn that he that touches Israel is counted as God's enemy (Gen 12:3; Jer 2:3; Zec 2:8-9; Is 10; Eze 25:1-7; Ob 1-21; Zep 2:8-11; 3:19). God's chastisement of His children for their sins is not unlike that of human parents in their discipline of their children for disobedience, which does not imply rejection, but, on the contrary, loving concern for them. Thus, God may allow some aggressive nation, such as Assyria or Babylonia, to chasten His people for their transgressions; but He will in turn punish the oppressor for his own sins (cf. Is 10:12f.). The Scriptures tell us to bless the Jews and to pray for the peace of Jerusalem, the promise being that God will in turn bless those who do so (Gen 12:3; Ps 122:6).

VERSE 20

"At that time will I bring you in, and at that time will I gather you; for I will make you a name and a praise among all the peoples of the earth, when I bring back your captivity before your eyes, saith the Lord" (v.20): this is as clear a promise of Israel's restoration as can be found in Scripture, and certainly in no sense was it realized at the first advent nor in Israel's first return from her captivity in Babylon. Israel's name was, and still is, a reproach throughout the earth; and this promise, given also in Deuteronomy 26:19, is yet to be fulfilled. Contrary to the present amillennial posture concerning the Scripture's promises of Israel's restoration, Israel in prophecy is not merely a type of the church, but she is a people eternally bound to God by virtue of the covenant made to Abraham (Ro 11:27). Their national restoration, as well as their spiritual renewal, is perhaps the most often repeated promise in Scripture, being set forth over 140 times (e.g. Lev 26:42-45; Deu 4: 27-31; 2 Sa 7:10; Joel 3:1f.; Amos 9:11-15; Ho 1:10-11; 2:14-23; 3:4-5; Is 2:1-4; 10:20-23; 11:10-16; 14:1-3; 27:12-13; 43:1-7; 49:13-26; Jer 3:14-19; 16:14-15; 23: 3-8; Eze 6:8-9; 20:33-44; 34:11-31; 36:1f.; 40-48; Mic 4:1-7; 7:9-20; Zec 2:4-13; 3:1-10; 8:1-23; 10:5-12; 12-14).

Israel, moreover, was given an eternal promise that the land of Palestine was to be her possession forever (Gen 12:1-7; 13:14-16; 15:1-21; 17:1-8; Ps 105:8-11; Eze 36; Amos 9:14-15). The promise of the restoration of Jerusalem, the holy city of Zion, to Israel is clearly predicted (e.g., in Is 2:1-4; Zec 2:4-5; 10-12; 8:1f; 14:1f; Lk 21: 24), while the return of the kingdom to Israel is set forth by Christ in Acts 1:6-7 (cf. Dan 7:27). Furthermore, Israel's ultimate salvation as a people is promised in Zechariah 12: 10-12, and the apostle Paul reiterates this truth in Romans 11. From this passage we are shown that the church is not Israel, nor does the church supplant Israel in God's covenant made to Abraham, for Israel is clearly addressed as a nation after the establishment of the church (Ro 10:1; 11; Ac 28:20). In Romans 11:25-29, God states that national Israel is only temporarily set aside until the full number of Gentiles are saved, after which he will restore Israel to her position. The resurrection of national Israel is also promised in Ezekiel 37, when David (Christ) will be King over them; and the two nations, Judah and Israel, will once again be united as one in their own land.

PART THREE
HABAKKUK

8

INTRODUCTION TO HABAKKUK

The Prophet

The prophet Habakkuk was a contemporary of Zephaniah and Jeremiah who also predicted at this time the Babylonian invasion of Judah and the destruction of Jerusalem. There is no reliable information concerning the prophet outside the book itself, which throws little light on the matter. However, numerous legends have grown up around his name. Some interpreters, connecting Isaiah 21:6 with Habakkuk 2:1, identify Habakkuk with the watchman set by Isaiah to watch for the fall of Babylon. The ancient rabbis connected the name Habakkuk, which means "embrace," with 2 Kings 4:16 ("Thou shalt embrace a son"), thus making him the son of the Shunammite woman in the time of Elisha.[1] Another claim is that he was a Levite. This theory is based upon the musical notation at the close of the third chapter (3:19) where the prophet directs that the psalm be sung accompanied by "my stringed instruments." Because of this it is surmised that he was qualified to participate in the temple music and would, therefore, have been of the tribe of Levi.[2]

The style of Habakkuk is unique. Instead of addressing the people directly as the Lord's spokesman, Habakkuk imparts his message as a dialogue between himself and God based upon certain questions which perplex him. The prophecy is divided into two parts. The first part, consisting of chapters 1-2, is the dialogue between the prophet and God concerning the Lord's announcement of the approaching judgment upon sinful Judah at the hands of the Babylonians. The second section, chapter 3, is a prayer in the form of a psalm. The psalm is a remembrance of the mighty works of the Lord in the past for His people, and a prayer for the Lord to revive His work on behalf of Israel.*

Period of Ministry

The period in which Habakkuk delivered his prophecy can be ascertained fairly accurately from the information given in the book itself. The time of the prophecy lies somewhere between the fall of Nineveh in 612 B.C. and the invasion of Judah in 605 B.C. (2 Ch 36:6-7). This is the period of the reign of Jehoiakim in Judah (609-597), after the death of Josiah at the hands of Pharoah-necoh in 609 B.C. (2 Ki 23:28-24:1). Assyria had been overthrown and was off the scene, and the Chaldeans seem to be just rising to power (1:6). Babylonia became the dominating power from 625-539 B.C. The description of the Chaldeans in 1:6-11 seems to indicate that they are on the scene and are engaged in swift and ruthless conquests, but have not as yet invaded Judah. The moral conditions described by Habakkuk in 1:2-4 indicate that it is a period of corruption and apostasy, which would be inconsistent with the time

* A *commentary* on chapters 1-2 of Habakkuk was discovered at Qumran (the location of a Jewish religious community). This commentary found among the Dead Sea Scrolls sets forth the religious sectarian views of the Essene community at Qumran about the first century B.C. For a discussion on this commentary see F.F. Bruce, *Biblical Exegesis in the Qumran Texts* and William LaSor, *Amazing Dead Sea Scrolls.*

of Josiah's reformation in 621 B.C. However, after Josiah's death the brief era of reform ended. Moreover, the phrase in 1:5 that judgment would befall Judah "in your days," would require a time after Josiah's reign (640-609), inasmuch as God had promised that this calamity would not occur during the days of Josiah (2 Ki 22:18ff.). In view of these considerations, a date of 609-605 B.C. seems likely for the prophecy.

Prior to the Babylonian rise to power, Assyria had controlled Mesopotamia, bringing Babylonia into subjection. Later Nabopolassar, a Chaldean, seized the kingship of Babylon and established an independent Chaldean empire known as the Neo-Babylonian Empire in 625 B.C. It was he who had joined in the destruction of Nineveh in 612 B.C., together with the Medes and Scythians. Egypt challenged the new Babylonian empire, and Pharoah-necoh marched to meet Nebuchadnezzar, the son of Nabopolassar, resulting in the defeat of the Egyptians in the Battle of Charchemish in 605 B.C. Nebuchadnezzar pursued the retreating Egyptians through Palestine, and subdued Jerusalem, taking numerous hostages, including Daniel. Josiah had been slain in 609 B.C. by Pharoah-necoh on his advance through Palestine to engage the Babylonians. After Josiah's death, Jehoahaz, Jehoiakim, Jehoiachin, and Zedekiah reigned on the throne of Judah in that order. Zedekiah, who had been promised support by the Egyptians, revolted against his Babylonian overlords after ten years. The Babylonians, as a result, again invaded Judah in 586 B.C., and after a long seige destroyed Jerusalem and the temple, and deported its citizens to Babylon as Habakkuk and Jeremiah had foretold.

The Purpose of the Prophecy

Upon the death of Josiah in 609 B.C., the period of reformation came to a close. In a short time the deplorable conditions of Manasseh's reign were once more to be found in Judah. Wickedness, corruption, oppression, and apostasy abounded. In such a situation the prophet is perplexed as to the reason why God allows such sin to go unpunished (1:2-4). The prophet is informed by God that Judah's punishment is forthcoming at the hands of His instrument of judgment, the ruthless Chaldeans (1:5-11). This perplexes Habakkuk further, inasmuch as he cannot understand how God, in his righteous justice, can use as an instrument of judicial punishment a nation more wicked and ruthless than Judah herself. What is the solution to this dilemma? The prophet decides to present the problem to the Lord and await an answer, which the Lord grants him (chap. 2).

God informs Habakkuk that evil is by its very nature self-destructive, whereas the righteous shall live by his faithfulness (2:4-20). The ruthless Chaldeans, proud in their strength, were unmindful of the fact that they were but God's instrument of chastisement upon sinful Judah, as Assyria had been in the case of the overthrow of the northern kingdom of Israel (Is 10). Habakkuk is told that the Chaldeans will, like Assyria, also be destroyed for their wickedness and for their oppression of Judah and the other nations.

On the other hand, faithfulness will characterize the life of the righteous man, who will exercise an abiding trust in God in the face of all adversity and trial, such as the calamity now confronting Judah. In this hour of trial, an unwavering trust in God and faithfulness to Him will alone give assurance of preservation to the righteous (cf Ps 91).

Outline of Habakkuk

I. The prophet's dilemma and God's solution, 1:1-2:20
   A. Habakkuk's first inquiry and God's reply, 1:1-11
      1. Why do Judah's iniquities remain unpunished? 1:1-4
      2. The divine solution: the Chaldean invasion, 1:5-11
   B. Habakkuk's second inquiry and God's reply, 1:12-2:20
      1. Why does God employ the wicked Chaldeans as His instrument of judgment? 1:12-17
      2. The divine solution: the Chaldeans' destruction, 2:1-20

II. The prophet's prayer, 3:1-19
   A. The prophet's petition, 3:1-2
   B. A theophany of judgment and deliverance, 3:3-15
   C. The prophet's meditation upon the vision, 3:16-19

9

THE PROPHET'S DILEMMA AND GOD'S SOLUTION
1:1—2:20

HABAKKUK'S FIRST INQUIRY AND GOD'S REPLY (1:1-11)

THE PROPHECY OPENS with an inquiry by Habakkuk concerning his perplexity because of the violence, iniquity, perverseness, and strife in Judah which seem to go unpunished by God (1:1-4). The Lord replies that His instrument of judgment, the Chaldeans, has been raised up for this purpose, and is even now on the march of conquest (1:5-11).

VERSE 1

"The burden which Habakkuk the prophet did see" (v.1): the superscription informs us of the method by which Habakkuk received his message. We are told that the prophet "saw" his prophecy, signifying that the form in which the revelation came was by vision. God opened the prophet's spiritual sight and unveiled before him the actual invasion of Judah by the Chaldeans, as well as the Babylonians' overthrow before the events occurred. This method of revelation upon which the prophets based their pronouncements is frequently seen in the Scriptures. Amos informs us that he received his prophecies by vision: "The words of Amos . . . which he saw concerning Israel" (Amos 1:1). So does Isaiah, whose superscription reads, "The vision of Isaiah . . . which he saw concerning Judah and Jerusalem" (Is 1:1). Note also the prophecies of Obadiah, Daniel, Ezekiel, Zechariah, and the apostle John (Revelation). This revelatory or prophetic state was a divinely induced condition whereby the prophet was enabled to see and hear things transcending the normal ability of the senses and intellect to perceive. This is in contrast to the self-induced trances and methods of divination resorted to by the sorcerers, mediums, and fortune tellers in their effort to communicate with the spirit world in order to obtain help or hidden information.

VERSES 2-4

The prophecy opens with Habakkuk's description of Judah's low moral and spiritual condition. "O Lord, how long shall I cry, and thou wilt not hear?" (v.2): the prophet states that he has long been crying out for divine intervention to correct the situation, but that God has not, as yet, answered his pleas. The prophet's moral sensibility is constantly being assaulted by the unchecked violence and iniquity, as well as Judah's constant violations of the law which he is compelled to witness (1:3-4). He is perplexed because of the widespread corruption which seems to go unpunished, urgently inquiring of the Lord, "How long shall I cry concerning their iniquity, before judgment is executed on the guilty?"

VERSES 5-11

"Behold . . . I am working a work in your days, which ye will not believe though it be told you. For, lo, I raise up the Chaldeans" (vv. 5-6): the description of the Chaldeans in verses 6-11 indicates that they are already on the world scene engaged in their conquests, but that they have not yet molested the Jews. Assyria had been recently overthrown, but it seemed unlikely at the time that Babylon would present any real threat to Judah. Evidence of this is seen in the fact that when Jeremiah, in the fourth year of Jehoiakim (605 B.C.), warned Judah of the destruction of Jerusalem in a few years at the hands of the Babylonians, it was considered so incredible that Jeremiah's announcement was looked upon by the Hebrews as an act of treason against the nation (Jer 36).

In answer to the prophet's pleas to punish the evildoers, God bids the prophet to look among the nations and He will show him one whom He will use to punish the iniquities of which Habakkuk complains. It is to be the Chaldeans. The prophet had asked, "How long?" God's reply is that it shall happen "in your days"—within the generation of those now living at the time of the prophecy.

The apostle Paul quotes the LXX (Septuagint) version of Habakkuk 1:5, giving its sense, in Acts 13:41, warning the Jews of the same fate that awaits them (at the hands of the Roman Empire) if they reject his message, as the unbelieving had done concerning Habakkuk's warning.

Jeremiah called the Chaldeans "an ancient nation" (Jer 5:15). They were a Semitic people who began to appear frequently in Mesopotamian records about 1000 B.C. and played a significant role in the political affairs of Babylonia for centuries, at times causing disaffection against Assyrian domination. About 625 B.C. Babylonia, under Nabopolassar, a Chaldean, established the Neo-Babylonian Empire, asserting its independence from Assyria and aiding in the destruction of Nineveh in 612 B.C.[1]

"The Chaldeans . . . march through the breadth of the earth, to possess dwelling-places that are not theirs" (v.6): the Babylonian armies were made up of vast hosts, composed not only of native troops, but also contingents from subject nations. They marched with great noise and tumult, spreading themselves far and wide over the countryside, plundering and destroying on all sides. Often they engaged their enemy in pitched battles, but generally they laid siege to the fortress cities of the enemy who had fled behind such defenses. These were assaulted with battering rams and by raising siege-mounds of dirt which would reach nearly to the tops of the walls of the city.[2]

"Their judgment and their dignity proceed from themselves" (v.7): the Chaldeans were subject to no one and ruled by their own might.

"Their horses also are swifter than leopards" (v.8): both Jeremiah and Ezekiel make reference to the swift horses and skilled horsemen of the Chaldeans who would ride against Judah (Jer 4:13; Eze 23:23).

"The set of their faces is forwards" (v.9): the Hebrew reads literally, "the assemblying of their faces is eastward," which is doubtless an idiomatic expression, signifying determination in accomplishing their purpose.

"Yea, he scoffeth at kings, and princes are a derision unto him" (v.10): this was certainly true of Nebuchadnezzar, as seen, for instance, in his treatment of Jehoiakim (2 Ch 36:6; 2 Ki 24:1-3; Jer 22:19), and Jehoiachin (2 Ki 24: 12, 15). "He derideth every stronghold; for he heapeth up dust": that is, he builds a siege-mound of dirt against the walls of the fortress cities and conquers them.

"Then shall he sweep by as a wind, and shall pass over, and be guilty, even he whose might is his god" (v.11): the meaning is that the Chaldeans in their sweeping conquests of Judah shall "pass over" (i.e., go beyond all restraint or exceed all limitations in cruelty and aggression), and thus become "guilty" by this conduct. Moreover, they are proud and arrogant because of their power, which has, in effect, become their "god."[3]

Thus, God's reply to the prophet concerning Judah's sin is that He is not indifferent to their prevailing ungodliness, for just retribution will surely come to the transgressors. The apparent delay in judgment does not arise from indifference and unconcern with regard to Judah's iniquity; but their chastisement awaits the appointed time, when the events of history have brought the proper circumstances together for its accomplishment. That God is in control of history is seen from the statement in verse 6, "I [will] raise up the Chaldeans," signifying that it is God who raises up the Neo-Babylonian Empire and sends it against other nations, including Judah to chasten her for her sins. This fact is asserted in Scripture repeatedly (cf. 1 Ki 11:14, 23; Amos 6:14; Is 10:5ff.; Nah 2:1ff.; Ro 9:17).

Habakkuk's Second Inquiry and God's Reply (1:12-2:20)

The use of the ruthless Chaldeans as ministers of divine punishment raises a new problem which perplexes the prophet: How can the Lord, whose eyes are too pure to look upon evil and oppression, appoint as His minister of justice and punishment the wicked and ruthless Chaldeans to swallow up Judah, who is by comparison more righteous than they? Are not the Chaldeans a proud idolatrous nation who gather up nations for brutal slaughter continually?

VERSES 12-17

"We shall not die" (v.12): the prophet begins his second inquiry with a confession of confidence that although God will chasten Israel, He will not destroy them (cf. Jer 46: 23).

"O Lord, thou hast ordained him for judgment; and . . . hast established him for correction. Thou that art of purer eyes than to behold evil, and that canst not look on perverseness, wherefore lookest thou upon them [the Chaldeans] that deal treacherously, and holdest thy peace when the wicked swalloweth up the man that is more righteous than he?" (vv. 12b-13): he then advances the problem which so perplexes him. "Why," he asks, "have the wicked Chaldeans been ordained as the instrument of judgment and correction for Israel?" This presents a profound theological problem to the prophet. Habakkuk cannot reconcile the problem of how God, who cannot look upon evil with complacency and cannot endure the sight of man's perverseness, can use such a wicked instrument as the Babylonians to punish Judah. Although Judah deserves chastening, her godless executioner of divine judgment is more wicked than she.

"Makest man as the fishes of the sea, as the creeping things, that have no ruler over them" (v.14): Habakkuk reminds the Lord of the wickedness of the Babylonian nation. The ruthless slaughter and conquests of the Babylonians leave the peoples of the plundered nations, whose leaders and armies have been destroyed and their defenses overthrown, as helpless as the swarming fish of the sea, or the lower forms of life in the earth.

"He taketh up all of them with the angle, he catcheth them in his net, and gathereth them in his drag" (v.15): Amos warned the apostate Israelites, concerning their coming captivity by the Assyrians, that "the days shall come upon you, that they shall take you away with hooks, and your residue with fish-hooks" (Amos 4:2). The term *angle* is also a reference to the use of such hooks, for it was the ancient practice of conquerors to put hooks in the nose or through the lips of their captives, attaching a rope or cord to this, and with their victims thus subdued, carry them away as slaves to their own country.* God warned Sennacherib, who had reviled the Jews and their God, "therefore will I put my hook in thy nose, and my bridle in thy lips, and will turn thee back by the way by which thou camest" (2 Ki 19:28; cf. 2 Ch 33:11, margin). "His net and . . . drag" refers to regular fishing nets, as well as large drag nets, from which nothing can escape. As "fishermen," the Chaldeans gather to themselves whole nations, plundering them, and bringing them under the yoke of Babylon, leaving nothing to escape their oppression.

"Therefore he sacrificeth unto his net, and burneth incense unto his drag; because by them his portion is fat and his food plenteous" (v.16): according to Herodotus, the Scythians and other heathen nations paid divine honors to their weapons; and Lange remarks that the Sarmatians were accustomed to offer annually a sacrifice to a sabre, which represented the insignia of Mars, the war god.[4]

"Shall he therefore empty his net, and spare not to slay the nations continually?" (v.17): Habakkuk restates his perplexity, after relating the ruthlessness and oppression of

* See p. 28 where an actual example of this is cited from one of Ashurbanipal's inscriptions.

the Chaldeans. It would seem, he surmises, that it is the wicked Chaldeans who need to be brought first under divine judgment and restraint, in order to put an end to their oppression of all the nations round about. Judah, although deserving chastisement, is but a small nation, not bent upon conquest and the oppression of other peoples. How then can God, who is righteous, permit the wicked Babylonians to remain unrestrained, to say nothing of using them as His instrument of chastisement against Judah? What is the solution to this dilemma?

CHAPTER 2, VERSES 1-5

The prophet's question is answered in chapter 2, where judgment upon the Chaldeans is pronounced.

"I will stand upon my watch, and set me upon the tower, and will look forth to see what he will speak with me" (v.1): unable to reconcile the problem, the prophet prepares himself to await further revelation concerning God's purpose in the providential use of the Chaldeans against Judah. The prophets often compared themselves to watchmen (cf. Is 21:8, 11; Jer 6:17; Eze 3:17; 33:2-3). In ancient times the watchman stationed himself upon the walls of the city, or in a watchtower, which enabled him to see in all directions and warn of approaching danger. The watchman was in a position to see all around and discern what was coming; Habakkuk, therefore, perhaps metaphorically using the figure of a watchman places himself apart on some watch-post, as it were, anxiously awaiting God's reply to his problem. Soon the solution comes in the form of a vision.

"And the Lord answered me, and said, Write the vision, and make it plain upon tablets, that he may run that readeth it. For the vision is yet for the appointed time, and it hasteth toward the end, and shall not lie: though it tarry, wait for it; because it will surely come, it will not delay" (vv.2-3): the vision is to be written down as as permanent record for others to read, as well as to confirm that Babylon's overthrow when it occurs was foretold by God. The phrase "that he may run that readeth it" does not signify, as some have supposed, that the message is to be so simple that a runner who hastens by may, without slowing his pace, be able to read it, or else the Hebrew would read "that he who runneth may read it." The intended meaning here is that the prophet is to make the message so plain that all who read it may then run to tell of the coming overthrow of the Chaldeans and deliverance of the faithful in Judah. The term "run" is used here in the sense of "run and announce the divine revelation."

God informs the prophet in verse 3 the reason for committing the prophecy to writing: its fulfillment is yet future; it "is yet for the appointed time." However, its certainty of fulfillment is stressed by the Lord, who encourages the prophet, as well as the faithful in Judah, not to be discouraged by any apparent delay in its accomplishment, for "though it tarry, wait for it; because it will surely come, it will not delay" (i.e., fail to be realized). The apostle Paul alludes to Habakkuk 2:3-4 in Hebrews 10:37-38, applying its sense to encourage those Jews, who were being tempted to give up their faith because of persecution, to hold fast. He admonishes them, saying that the faithful Jews will wait for the fulfillment of God's promise to them, although it may appear to be delayed for a time; whereas the unfaithful will "shrink back" and give up their confession of faith.

"Behold, his soul is puffed up, it is not upright in him;

but the righteous shall live by his faith" (v.4): after God gives the prophet instructions concerning the preparation for preservation and communication of the forthcoming revelation, He then unveils the message of consolation: *The just shall live in his faithfulness; whereas the proud and wicked shall perish* (vv.4-20). Thus, the revelation unfolds a universal, spiritual principle, which is applicable to all men in every dispensation. The essence of sin is pride, especially as it expresses itself in self-exaltation and arrogant self-confidence, as in the case of the ruthless and powerful Chaldean Empire under Nebuchadnezzar, whom God used to punish Judah. Daniel records how that God humbled the great king, who boasted, "Is not this great Babylon, which I have built for the royal dwelling-place, by the might of my power and for the glory of my majesty?" (Dan 4:30). Divine judgment fell upon the king, humbling and abasing him, until he was compelled to acknowlcdge that God ruled in the kingdoms of the earth, as well as in heaven, and that "those that walk in pride he is able to abase" (Dan 4:37).

After the iniquities of Judah have been punished, God will turn His attention to their oppressors, the Chaldeans, and punish that wicked nation, for "behold his soul is puffed up, it is not upright in him." The Babylonian nation, although seeming to prosper in its course of ruthless conquest for the present, is merely executing God's righteous judgments; but it is proud and haughty, and thus the nation is not upright before God and will be punished. However, let him who is faithful take courage, declares God, for he shall be delivered and live by virtue of his faithfulness, whereas the proud and arrogant carries within himself the seeds of destruction.

The apostle Paul cites Habakkuk 2:4 in Romans 1:17 translating it, "the righteous shall live by faith." The effect of this verse upon the life of Martin Luther (and subsequent Protestantism) is without question one of the most significant episodes in religious history.

Although he had prepared for a career in law, Luther earnestly sought spiritual security and entered a monastery, hoping to find inner peace and the assurance of his forgiveness. He was disappointed in his spiritual quest in spite of the fact that he searched for God's approval by every means: monastic service, fastings, prayers, self-punishment, and confession. Disillusioned by the conviction that man could not earn salvation either by means of good works or the sacraments, he suffered periods of extreme spiritual depression.

It was while preparing a series of lectures on the book of Romans in 1513 that the phrase, "the righteous shall live by faith" (1:17), brought home to him the truth of *justification by faith,* which became the basis of Protestantism. It is through faith in Jesus Christ and His shed blood for man's sins, Luther saw, that the sinner finds forgiveness, peace, and eternal salvation. Justification is by faith alone.[5]

When the Scriptures inform us that "the righteous shall live by faith" (Hab 2:4; Ro 1:17; Gal 3:11), this is not meant to be limited to the initial salvation experience but implies that the believer has been called to "live by faith" in regard to his daily life as well, trusting in God in every way and for everything. The importance of total faith in the life of the believer is clearly indicated in the Scriptures, for we are told that "without faith it is impossible to be well-pleasing unto him" (Heb 11:6), and that "whatsoever is not of faith is sin" (Ro 14:23). God's reply to Habakkuk teaches that *the righteous man exercises an abiding trust in God in the face of all adversity and trial, as well as in every circumstance of life.*

God informs us that He has made provision through Christ's work at Calvary for the believer's every need, whether spiritual or temporal, as well as for the effective accomplishment of the work He has commissioned the church to perform. The Scriptures are filled with divine promises, assurances, rights, and privileges based upon Christ's atonement which are to be appropriated by faith (e.g., Ps 37; 91; 121; Mt 6:33; 18:19; 21:22; Mk 11:22-24; 16:15-20; Lk 11:13; Ac 2:38-39; Jn 14:14; Phil 4:13, 19; Heb 10:23; 11:1; 13:6; Ja 5:14-16; 3 Jn 2). The life of faith is based upon the confidence that God is faithful to do all that He has pledged Himself to do in His Word (Num 23:19; Heb 10:23).

The Lord's reply to Habakkuk teaches, in the second place, that the righteous man is a faithful man, for verse 4 in the Hebrew reads literally: "the righteous [man] shall live by his faithfulness." This was the Hebrew concept of faith—faithfulness. Justifying faith results in faithfulness to God and His commandments. It is significant that there was no word for *faith* in the Hebrew language. The term does not occur in the original Hebrew in the Old Testament (only in the English translations). This does not mean, of course, that faith was unknown to the Hebrews or that the saints of the Old Testament dispensation were not also, like New Testament saints, justified by faith. On the contrary, we are told that Abraham was justified by his faith in God. We are informed in Genesis 15:6: "He believed in the Lord; and he reckoned it to him for righteousness." Nevertheless, the Hebrew language had no term for faith. *Faith* is an abstract term which needs to be explained or interpreted in order to be properly understood. Hence, the term which expressed the Old Testament saint's trust in God was *faithfulness*. The Hebrew language is graphic and picturesque, and this term described for the Jew what one does who has faith in God: he is faithful. This term characterized the life of the man who confessed "I believe God."

Although in the New Testament the apostle Paul translates Habakkuk 2:4 (in Romans 1:17) as "the righteous shall live by faith," using the Greek term *faith* for the Hebrew word for faithfulness, the apostle, nevertheless, as an Israelite, reiterates repeatedly the Hebrew concept of faith in his epistles; namely, *faithfulness*. He stresses the fact that justifying faith always produces faithfulness (e.g., Ro 6; Eph 2:8-10). Throughout the New Testament, the Hebrew conception of faith as faithfulness is set forth; and the principle that justifying faith is incompatible with unfaithfulness or disobedience appears again and again.

"Yea, moreover, wine is treacherous, a haughty man, that keepeth not at home; who enlargeth his desire as Sheol, and is as death, and cannot be satisfied, but gathereth unto him all nations, and heapeth unto him all peoples" (v.5): the sense is that strong drink is a primary cause of the Chaldeans' pride or haughtiness, inciting them to leave their home to engage in their lust for conquest, which, like Sheol (place of departed dead) and death, cannot be satisfied. Sheol is called insatiable (Pro 27:20; 30:16; Is 5:14). Love for wine was one of the besetting sins of the Babylonians, often begetting a proud contempt, and was, in the case of Belshazzar and his feast, an immediate cause of the downfall of Babylon (Dan 5; cf. Pro 20:1; 23:29-35).

VERSES 6-20

Shall not the oppressed nations take up a parable against the Chaldean nation, and utter a taunting proverb against him, pronouncing just retribution upon the ruthless conqueror? asks God. The proverb given by Habakkuk against the Babylonians depicting their destruction consists of five dire woes, and, uttered in derision, is a taunting poem consisting of five stanzas of three verses each.

1. *Woe because of their plunder, bloodshed, and violence* (vv.6-8). "Shall not all these take up a parable against him?" (v.6) refers to the nations oppressed by the Chaldeans. "Ladeth himself with pledges": the KJV mistranslates *pledge* by "thick clay." In the Old Testament a pledge consisted of some personal property of a debtor, which he gave as security against the payment he owed. Abuses of the pledge are censured (Amos 2:8; Ex 22:26-27). The meaning intended here seems to be that the Chaldean nation is to be compared to a harsh usurer, who is busily acquiring the property of others either by plunder or by exacting tribute. This great quantity of treasure being amassed is regarded as an accumulation of pledges, a burden of debt which one day must be restored, inasmuch as the Chaldeans themselves shall be plundered by those nations whom they now oppress (vv.7-8). It is the law of just retribution which shall bring this about, which was enunciated earlier by the prophet Obadiah, who said, "as thou hast done, it shall be done unto thee; thy dealing shall return upon thine own head" (Ob 15).

2. *Woe because of their avarice, pride, and cruelty* (vv. 9-11). "Woe to him that getteth an evil gain for his house" (v.9): the "house" is, of course, not only the royal house or Chaldean dynasty, but also the nation itself (v.10). The

Babylonian empire had deluded itself into thinking itself secure because of its great towering fortifications ("that he may set his nest on high"), built as a result of its plunder. The formidable walls and defenses of the Chaldeans had given them a false sense of security, with the result that they considered themselves impregnable. The phrase "set his nest on high" is a figurative expression occurring elsewhere in Scripture, always denoting sinful pride, or arrogant self-confidence and security (Num 24:21-22; Ob 3-4). "Thou hast devised shame to thy house, by cutting off many peoples" (v.10): the same means by which the Chaldeans obtained their power and sense of security shall be their ruin. "For the stone shall cry out of the wall, and the beam out of the timber shall answer it" (v.11): this is a proverbial expression denoting the depth of their crimes against mankind deserving punishment; even inanimate objects shall raise their voice, as it were, to denounce the Babylonian cruelty, as if the very structures built by rapine would testify against them. (Note Luke 19:40 for a similar expression.)

3. *Woe because of their bloodshed and iniquity* (vv.12-14). "Woe to him that buildeth a town with blood, and establisheth a city by iniquity" (v.12): like the Assyrians, the ruthlessness and cruelty of the Chaldeans is well attested to by the ancient historians. They massacred the inhabitants of conquered cities by fire, sword, and impalement; they mutilated their prisoners, executed the children, and carried whole populations captive. The Babylonians, after successful expeditions, enlarged their cities and enriched their temples and palaces with the spoils and plunder of other nations. "The peoples labor for the fire" (v.13): the Chaldeans have labored in vain, God declares, for they

have gathered plunder and raised up their palaces, temples, and cities only to supply fuel for the coming fire in their destruction. Jeremiah announced identical judgment upon Babylon (Jer 51:58). Babylon, the type of hostile world power opposed to God, must be destroyed; "for the earth shall be filled with the knowledge of the glory of the Lord" (v.14). This announcement looks to the establishment of the millennial kingdom. Isaiah also portrays this day using the same expression, looking forward to the glorious age to come when "the wolf shall dwell with the lamb, and . . . they shall not hurt nor destroy in all my holy mountain; for the earth shall be full of the knowledge of the Lord" (Is 11:6-10). It is obvious that the fulfillment of this prophecy is yet future, when godless world power and all oppression have been overthrown (Dan 2:44) and the whole earth comes under the reign and lordship of Jesus Christ (Is 2:1-4; Zec 14:9).

4. *Woe because of their debauchery of others, as well as their wholesale devastation* (vv. 15-17). "Woe unto him that giveth his neighbor drink . . . that thou mayest look on their nakedness" (v.15): they are charged with leading subject nations into debauchery, and adding their own vices and perversions ("that addest thy venom"), in order to debase and humiliate them. "Drink thou also, and be as one uncircumcised" (v.16): they shall receive in kind the same ignominy and shame with which they debased and humiliated others. To be uncircumcised marked one as a Gentile or heathen and outside God's covenant; here it expresses God's utter contempt for Judah's oppressors and indicates the climax of their coming degradation. "For the violence done to Lebanon shall cover thee" (v.17): if taken literally, this would refer to the wholesale devasta-

tion inflicted by the Babylonians upon the choice and valuable cedars of Lebanon (Is 14:8; 37:24). Babylon will suffer the same destruction as the forests of Lebanon. Some interpreters take it to be a figurative reference to Palestine as a whole, or to Jerusalem in particular, which suffered at the hands of the Babylonians. The parable in Ezekiel 17 equates Lebanon with Jerusalem and its cedars with people, whom Babylon will cut down and carry away. "The destruction of the beasts, which made them afraid": again, if the phrase is to be taken literally, it indicates that the same destruction of the wild animals of Lebanon by the Babylonians, and the consequent fear, shall be inflicted upon them. If figurative, then the prophet is saying in effect, "as you hunted down men as wild beasts, so will be the retributive punishment of Babylon by others."

5. *Woe because of their idolatry* (vv.18-20). "What profiteth the graven image?" (v.18): the final woe is introduced with a question concerning the value of trusting in pagan gods of wood and stone. The Chaldeans trusted in their man-made gods, giving them credit for their victories. However, they will not be able to save them from the approaching destruction; therefore, what good are they? Translating verse 18 freely, it would read, "What profit is there in graven images? for they are man-made. The molten image is a teacher of lies. He that fashions it is trusting in dumb idols." "Woe unto him that saith to the wood, Awake; to the dumb stone, Arise!" (v.19): both Jeremiah and Isaiah describe the folly of those who attribute divine powers and attributes to the creations made with their own hands (Is 44:9-20; Jer 10:1-5). "But the Lord is in his holy temple: let all the earth keep silence before him" (v.20): the prophet, in conclusion, contrasts the living

God of Israel, who has the power to save or destroy, with the dumb idol-gods of the heathen; therefore, let all the earth give reverence unto Him (i.e., "be silent" before His presence). The Hebrew term is the same as in Zephaniah 1:7, literally, *Hush!*

10

THE PROPHET'S PRAYER
3:1-19

THE PROPHET'S PETITION (3:1-2)

ON THE BASIS of the revelation just given him concerning the chastisement of Judah and the destruction of the Babylonian empire, the prophet confesses his fear at the report; whereupon he is constrained to plead that the Lord would, with regard to Judah's punishment, in His wrath also show mercy and once more revive His work in behalf of His people (3:1-2). In answer to his prayer, the Lord appears in a majestic theophanic vision. The psalm recalls past instances when God vindicated His people and overthrew their enemies.

VERSES 1-2

"A prayer of Habakkuk the prophet" (v.1): chapter 3 is a prayer in the form of a poem. The name and title are given to indicate that this is not a private prayer but is given by the prophet under divine inspiration. "Set to Shigionoth," indicating the type of rhythm the ode is to be sung to (in this instance, as a song of triumph).

"O Lord, I have heard the report of thee, and am afraid" (v.2): the prophet's formal prayer is found in verse 2, the rest of the poem being devotional. The fearful report to which he refers is the revelation in chapter 2, concerning Judah's coming chastisement and the overthrow of Babylon. "O Lord, revive thy work in the midst of the years. . . . in wrath remember mercy": the prophet's prayer is a plea for God to keep His covenant with Israel in mind when He sends the ruthless Chaldeans against Judah to chasten her for her sins. In her period of exile and punishment, let the Lord remember her and begin to deal once more with her as His chosen nation. It is in this way that mercy can be demonstrated in the midst of judicial wrath.

A Theophany of Judgment and Deliverance (3:3-15)

In answer to the prophet's petition, he receives a glorious revelation of God. The imagery in the vision is based upon the accounts of God's mighty works of deliverance on behalf of His people in ancient times, and His judgments upon their enemies in Egypt, at the Red Sea, at Sinai, and in the conquest under Joshua in Canaan. The splendor of the theophany is first described (vv.3-4); then the prophet sets forth the purpose and effects of the Lord's appearance: He comes once more to judge and punish the nations and deliver His people as in days of old (vv.5-15). Israel's deliverance from Egypt under the mighty hand of God also typifies her liberation from Babylon, as well as her future deliverance from the nations at the close of the age (Joel 3; Zec 14).

The prophet's contemplation of divine judgment produces, at first, fear at the prospect of God's chastisement of Judah (vv.16-17); nevertheless, on behalf of the nation, Habakkuk expresses faith in the ultimate salvation of God when the present period of chastisement is over (vv. 18-19).

VERSES 3-4

"God came from Teman, and . . . from mount Paran" (v.3): God is depicted as coming from the region south of Judah in judgment and deliverance. "Teman" in Hebrew means "south" and is also the name of a city of Edom, the country lying south of Judah. "Mount Paran" signifies the desert region south of Judah extending to Sinai. In Deuteronomy 33:2 and Judges 5:4, God is depicted as coming up from these regions, which signified in a general way to the Hebrew that the Lord's approach was from Sinai, where He had entered into covenant with His people.

"And his brightness was as the light . . . and there was the hiding of his power" (v.4): there, in that glorious light surrounding His Person, was the hiding place of His majesty. He clothes Himself with light as a garment (Ps 104:2), veiling His unsurpassing glory, as no mortal may look upon Him in the fulness of His splendor and live (1 Ti 6:16).

VERSES 5-15

After describing the glory and splendor of the appearance of the Lord, Habakkuk next turns to the purpose: *God comes in judgment to deliver His people.*

"Before him went the pestilence" (v.5): this recalls the ten plagues upon the Egyptians in behalf of Israel's deliverance (Ex 7-11; cf. Zec 14:12-15, in the latter days). "And fiery bolts [burning coals] went forth at his feet": no doubt this refers to His majestic appearance at Sinai (Ex 19:16f.).

"He stood, and measured the earth" (v.6): He surveyed it in preparation for judgment, for "He beheld, and drove asunder the nations," delivering them into the hands of His people (the Egyptians, Amalekites, and the nations of Palestine; cf. Is 14:1-3; Zec 2:9); "and the eternal mountains were scattered," as even the emblems of stability and permanence quake at His advance (as at Sinai, Ex 19; and at the second advent, Rev 16; Zec 14:3-5). "His goings were as of old" (margin: His ways are everlasting) signifies that, as God acted in behalf of His people in the past in their deliverance from Egypt, so He will act in the future.

"I saw the tents of Cushan in affliction; the curtains [tent curtains] of the land of Midian did tremble" (v.7): the nations on both sides of God's advance fall into fear and confusion, as in Israel's advance from Egypt (Ex 15: 14-16). "Cushan" (Ethiopia) and "Midian" (land east of the Red Sea) are named as signifying that the nations on the west and east of the Red Sea tremble at His advance.

"Was the Lord displeased with the rivers . . . or thy wrath against the sea?" (v.8): was God's anger against inanimate nature when He sent plagues upon the Nile River, and parted the Red Sea? The answer is implied in the next phrase, "thy chariots of salvation," for He demonstrated His power over creation in order to effect the salvation of His people.

"Thy bow was made quite bare [i.e., uncovered for use]; the oaths to the tribes were a sure word" (v.9): the oaths include His covenant and promises, beginning with Abraham (cf. Ro 11:25f.). "Thou didst cleave the earth with rivers" is perhaps a reference to bringing forth water from the rock for His people (Ex 17:6; Num 20:10-11), or as a consequence of an earthquake attending His advance (v.6).

"The mountains saw thee, and were afraid" (v.10): Mount Sinai quaked (Ex 19:18; Ps 114). "The tempest of waters passed by": at the Red Sea and the Jordan, God caused the waters to pass away before the advance of His people. "The deep uttered its voice, and lifted up its hands on high": this figure signifies that, as men by utterance and gesture indicate submission, so did the elements at God's rebuke.

"The sun and the moon stood still in their habitation" (v.11): an obvious reference to the divine intervention on Joshua's behalf once again portrays God's sovereign control of creation, which He commands and regulates in order to effect the deliverance of His people (cf. Mt 24:29-31). "At the light of thine arrows as they went, at the shining of thy glittering spear": the Hebrew omits "as." The reference seems to be to the flight of Joshua's enemies as a result of hailstorms, perhaps accompanied with lightnings (Jos 10: 10-11). Lightnings in Scripture are sometimes called God's "arrows" (Ps 18:14; 77:17).

"Thou didst march through the land in indignation; Thou didst thresh the nations in anger" (v.12): it was not the military prowess of Israel, but the presence of the Lord which accounted for her great victories over her enemies (Ex 23:20-23; Deu 33:29), as it will in her future deliverance from Babylon ("the Lord stirred up the spirit of Cyrus," Ezra 1:1), as well as in the end times (Zec 14:3f.).

"Thou wentest forth for the salvation of thy people . . . thine anointed" (v.13): that was on behalf of Israel, who is called God's "anointed ones" in Scripture: "He suffered no man to do them wrong; yea, he reproved kings for their sakes, saying, Touch not mine anointed ones" (Ps 105:14-15; Zec 2:8-9). "Thou woundedst the head out of the house of the wicked man": the figure describes the Babylonian kingdom and its king, which God will destroy. Some suggest, not unlikely, that this is also an allusion to the future overthrow of Antichrist (cf. Ps 69:21; 110:6). "Laying bare the foundation even unto the neck": the destruction will be complete—from top to bottom.

"Thou didst pierce with his own staves the head of his warriors" (v.14): the leaders were slain with their own spears or weapons. "They came as a whirlwind to scatter me": that refers to Israel, with whom the prophet here identifies himself (cf. 1:12).

"Thou didst tread the sea with thy horses, the heap of mighty waters" (v.15): the theophany concludes with a return to the time of the Exodus and Israel's deliverance from her enemies. God is portrayed as a great Warrior leading His troops through the sea to the promised land.

The Prophet's Meditation upon the Vision (3:16-19)

The terrible vision of the Lord coming in judgment upon the earth produces fear at the prospect of His chastisement of Israel (vv.16-17); nevertheless, remembering God's word that "the righteous man shall live in his faithfulness," the prophet expresses steadfast faith in the ultimate salvation of God when the present affliction is past (vv.18-19).

VERSE 16

"I heard, and my body trembled . . . because I must wait quietly for the day of trouble, for the coming up of the people that invadeth us" (v.16): the "invaders" clearly refer to the invading Chaldeans, mentioned in chapters 1-2. In 2:1, Habakkuk is seen awaiting God's reply to his perplexing questions; and in 3:2, he makes reference to the Lord's reply (given in 2:4-20), saying, "I have heard the report . . . and am afraid." The vision of God's power and splendor, demonstrated in overthrowing Israel's enemies in the past, produces fright in the prophet's heart as he contemplates the "report" of Israel's judicial punishment at the hands of the Babylonians. The punishment of Judah for her sins is decreed; and the prophet, who has had his spiritual vision opened to her inevitable judgment, can do nothing now but await the execution of her sentence at the appointed time.

VERSES 17-19

"For though the fig-tree shall not flourish" (v.17): the conquering nations often devastated the land of the people they invaded (cf. Deu 20:19-20) and destroyed the herds and flocks.

"Yet I will rejoice in the Lord, I will joy in the God of my salvation" (v.18): in spite of the fact that the Babylonian invasion soon to come would leave the land bare and devastated, the prophet, in behalf of Israel, expresses hope of salvation and of ultimate restoration.

"He maketh my feet like hinds' feet, and will make me to walk upon my high places" (v.19): speaking on behalf of Israel, Habakkuk expresses his confidence that God will restore the nation's life and joy (under the figure of the nimble deer or hind). The high places are called "mine" to imply that Israel will be restored to her own land, a land of hills.

Thus, the prophet having begun his prayer with fear and trembling as a result of the "report" which the Lord had given him concerning the nation's punishment at the hands of the ruthless Chaldeans, concludes (as did Zephaniah) on a note of triumph, confessing his faith in Israel's final salvation and restoration to her land.

NOTES

Nahum

CHAPTER 1

1. For a discussion on the date of Nahum, see Walter A. Maier, *The Book of Nahum: A Commentary.*

2. C. F. Keil and F. Delitzsch, "The Twelve Minor Prophets," in *Biblical Commentary on the Old Testament,* 2:4.

CHAPTER 2

1. Robert Jamieson, A. R. Fausset, and David Brown, *A Commentary, Critical and Explanatory, on the Old and New Testaments,* 1:729.

CHAPTER 3

1. Robert Jamieson et.al., *A Commentary . . . on the Old and New Testaments,* 1:730.
2. Merrill F. Unger, *Unger's Bible Dictionary,* p. 91.
3. Austin H. Layard, *Nineveh and Its Remains,* pp. 281-86.
4. F. Lenormant and E. Chevallier, "Rise and Fall of Assyria," in *The Great Events by Famous Historians,* 1:114.
5. Daniel D. Luckenbill, *Ancient Records of Assyria and Babylonia,* 2:419-20.

CHAPTER 4

1. George Rawlinson, *The Seven Great Monarchies of the Ancient Eastern World,* 1:278-80.
2. D. D. Luckenbill, *Ancient Records of Assyria and Babylonia,* 1:148.
3. Ibid., 1:213.
4. Ibid., 2:319, 304.
5. Ibid., 1:146-47.
6. For an up-to-date, comprehensive exposition of the subject, see Hobart E. Freeman, *Angels of Light?* (Claypool, Ind.: Faith, 1969).
7. Robert Jamieson et al., *A Commentary . . . on the Old and New Testaments,* 1:732.

Zephaniah

CHAPTER 5

1. W. J. Deane, "Introduction to the Book of Zephaniah," in *The Pulpit Commentary,* ed. H. D. M. Spence and Joseph S. Exell, 14:ii-iii.
2. Frederick C. Eisenlen, "Zephaniah, Book of," in *The International Standard Bible Encyclopedia,* ed. James Orr, 5:3144.

CHAPTER 6

1. For a comprehensive and scholarly study on the Christian's attitude toward the world and its practices, as reflected in the early church, see C. J. Cadoux, *The Early Church and the World* (Edinburgh: T. & T. Clark, 1955).

2. Hobart E. Freeman, *An Introduction to the Old Testament Prophets,* pp. 217-19.

3. Merrill F. Unger, *Unger's Bible Dictionary,* p. 97.

CHAPTER 7

1. R. A. Torrey, *What the Bible Teaches,* pp. 271-78.

2. Edward J. Young, *An Introduction to the Old Testament,* pp. 247-48.

3. A. E. Gaebelien, *The Prophet Joel,* p. 136.

4. John Peter Lange, "Zephaniah," in *Commentary on the Holy Scriptures,* trans. Philip Schaff, p. 32.

5. H. E. Freeman, *An Introduction to the Old Testament Pröphets,* pp. 308-24.

HABAKKUK

CHAPTER 8

1. Frederick C. Eiselen, *The Minor Prophets,* pp. 463-64.

2. C. F. Keil and F. Delitzsch, *Biblical Commentary on the Old Testament,* 2:49.

CHAPTER 9

1. Jack Finegan, *Light from the Ancient Past,* pp. 183-84.

2. George Rawlinson, *The Seven Great Monarchies of the Ancient Eastern World,* 2:216.

3. Robert Jamieson et al., *A Commentary . . . on the Old and New Testaments,* 1:734.

4. John Peter Lange, "Habakkuk," in *Commentary on the Holy Scriptures,* p. 21.

5. Kenneth Scott Latourette, *A History of Christianity,* pp. 703-7.

BIBLIOGRAPHY

Bruce, F. F. *Biblical Exegesis in the Qumran Texts.* Grand Rapids: Eerdmans, 1959.

Deane, W. J. "Introduction to the Book of Zephaniah." In *The Pulpit Commentary,* vol. 14. Ed. H. D. M. Spence and Joseph S. Excell. Grand Rapids: Eerdmans, 1950.

Eiselen, Frederick Carl. *The Minor Prophets.* New York: Eaton & Mains, 1907.

———. "Zephaniah, Book of." In *The International Standard Bible Encyclopedia,* ed. James Orr. Vol. 5. Grand Rapids: Eerdmans, 1946.

Finegan, Jack. *Light from the Ancient Past.* Princeton: Princeton U., 1954.

Freeman, Hobart E. *An Introduction to the Old Testament Prophets.* Chicago: Moody, 1971.

Gaebelien, A. C. *The Prophet Joel.* New York: Our Hope, 1909.

Jamieson, Robert; Fausset, A. R.; and Brown, David. *A Commentary, Critical and Explanatory, on the Old and New Testaments.* Vol. 1. Glasgow: Collins, 1895.

Keil, C. F., and Delitzsch, F. *Biblical Commentary on the Old Testament,* trans. James Martin. Vol. 2. Grand Rapids: Eerdmans, 1954.

Lange, John Peter. *Commentary on the Holy Scriptures,* trans. Philip Schaff. Grand Rapids: Zondervan, n.d.

Latourette, Kenneth Scott. *A History of Christianity.* New York: Harper, 1953.

LaSor, William S. *Amazing Dead Sea Scrolls.* Chicago: Moody, 1956.

Layard, Austen H. *Nineveh and Its Remains*. New York: Putnam, 1852.

Lenormant, F., and Chevallier, E. "Rise and Fall of Assyria." In *The Great Events by Famous Historians,* ed. R. Johnson. Vol. 1. New York: National Alumni, 1914.

Luckenbill, Daniel D. *Ancient Records of Assyria and Babylonia*. Vols. 1 & 2. Chicago: U. of Chicago, 1926.

Maier, Walter A. *The Book of Nahum: A Commentary*. St. Louis: Concordia, 1959.

Rawlinson, George. *The Seven Great Monarchies of the Ancient Eastern World*. Vols. 1 & 2. New York: Millar, 1885.

Torrey, R. A. *What the Bible Teaches*. New York: Revell, n.d.

Unger, Merrill F. *Unger's Bible Dictionary*. Chicago: Moody, 1962.

Young, Edward J. *An Introduction to the Old Testament*. Grand Rapids: Eerdmans, 1954.